S Ioh[ns]

Trinity College

Trinity college chapell

All Hallowes in the Iury

S Sepulchre

S Michael

High Streete

Bridge streete

Gray ffreers

Shoemaker Lane

Trinity church

Trsus

KING'S COLLEGE CHAPEL, CAMBRIDGE

KING'S COLLEGE CHAPEL, CAMBRIDGE

The story and the renovation

by

RODNEY TIBBS

Foreword by Sir Martyn Beckett Bt, M.C., B.A., A.R.I.B.A.

TERENCE DALTON LIMITED

LAVENHAM   SUFFOLK

1970

Published by
TERENCE DALTON LIMITED
S B N 900963 17 4

Photo Engravings by
STAR ILLUSTRATION WORKS LIMITED

Printed in Great Britain at

THE LAVENHAM PRESS LIMITED
LAVENHAM   SUFFOLK

To Sheila

CONTENTS

INDEX OF ILLUSTRATIONS

ACKNOWLEDGEMENT

IT WAS WHILE working on the details of the renovation and redesign of the east end of King's College Chapel for a special supplement for the Cambridge Evening News that I realised I had an abundance of riches on my hands. The Chapel is one of the world's finest monuments in architecture and the scheme which the College has completed is the most comprehensive in the Chapel's 500 years history.

There were exciting discoveries, intensive investigations and many hours of loving and painstaking work by modern craftsmen whose skill complemented that of their forebears. As a result the Chapel now presents the same crispness of carving and mellowness of tone it must have possessed immediately after its completion.

This is not a history book or a guide book. It is purely a personal attempt to chronicle some of the most important changes in the Chapel's long and distinguished history. To do this I have found myself writing about modern craftsmen, and in order to put their efforts into correct perspective, a certain amount of historical background has been introduced. I am hopeful that the book will enrich a visit to the Chapel and encourage those who have never stepped inside the building to accept that the sound of its famous choir is more than matched by the beauty of the fabric.

Without the assistance of many people a book like this cannot begin. Sir Martyn Beckett the architect for the entire scheme has been more than generous with advice and guidance. I trespassed to a considerable extent upon his time and will always remain in his debt. In addition to the introduction to this book he also provided a considerable amount of basic data and material and gives us a valuable peep into his thoughts by allowing the reproduction of early sketches for his altar scheme which he subsequently rejected.

Joyce Conway Evans whose superb skill as a designer can be judged from the magnificence of the altar frontal which she created for the Chapel is an equally gifted artist. She readily gave permission for one of her works to be used on the cover of this book and in so doing made a vital contribution to its appearance.

King's College itself is in no way associated with this book but it would be churlish to ignore the most valuable assistance and guidance provided by many members of the College and its library and Chapel staff.

I must also thank Mr Roy Hardwick of Messrs Rattee and Kett. He and his firm have been looking after the Chapel fabric for many years and there can be few men with greater knowledge of its structure. The same can be said of Mr Dennis King, that noted authority on stained glass. Kings of Norwich worked miracles with the famous and priceless windows of the Chapel during the course of the renovation and gave me the full run of their workshops as they did so.

Others provided such important guidance and information that without them the task would have been impossible. They include Mr J. D. Briggs, headmaster of the King's College Choir School, Mr Michael Goodchild, the school's indefatigable and enthusiastic amateur historian, Mr E. B. Ceadel, the University Librarian and his staff and the Royal Commission on Historical Monuments.

Among the mass of material made available to me during the course of research for the book were a number of superb photographs. I would like to express my appreciation of work by Ramsey and Muspratt of Cambridge and Mr Edward Leigh, to John Redman who took a number of special pictures for the book, and to the Cambridge Evening News and The Times for permission to reproduce some outstanding examples of their work.

By the Same Author

FENLAND RIVER

The Story of the Great Ouse
and its tributaries

Published by

TERENCE DALTON LIMITED
LAVENHAM   SUFFOLK

Sir Martyn Beckett, Bt., M.C., B.A., A.R.I.B.A., the architect chosen by King's College to undertake the redesign of the east end of the chapel as a setting for Rubens' "Adoration of the Magi". He also supervised the restoration work. *Cambridge Evening News*

FOREWORD

HERE IS a book that places King's College Chapel in the perspective of history and as one of the great architectural achievements in the world.

Mr. Tibbs describes its background history, architectural features, together with chapters on the glass, the organ, and the choir school. He also tells in some detail of the recent renovations and innovations in which I was involved.

To rearrange the interior of such a building was a daunting prospect and was bound to provide strong reactions from many people of diverse opinions. Discussion will last, as Mr. Tibbs points out, as long as the Chapel does. Once the proposals had been approved however, the problem was to integrate the whole of the work and to complete it within ten months. In the event this was done with two weeks to spare, and is to the credit of all who worked upon it.

The awe and admiration which anyone must feel on entering the Chapel inspired our present day craftsmen to match the skill of Wastell and his contemporaries. In this they did not fail. As a miracle in stone and glass the Chapel stands today, and lets hope for years to come, as one of the supreme monuments to God and the human spirit.

Sir Martyn Beckett, Bt., M.C., B.A., A.R.I.B.A.
London, S.W.7.   June, 1970.

INTRODUCTION

ONE MAY excusably wonder, as I did, how a building, people and a picture, by some strange decision of nature, can become a perfect partnership. It was, I found, an odd law of physics by which King's College Chapel and more than 80,000 visitors it receives each year combine to provide the right humidity conditions in which to site Ruben's magnificent "Adoration of the Magi".

As the result of a thorough and extensive programme of restoration to the building fabric costing over £150,000, the interior of the Chapel now looks at its finest for many hundreds of years, possibly since it was originally built, and the treatment of its east end has been specifically arranged to house the Rubens' altarpiece. But it was not until detailed investigations, which preceded the scheme, were carried out that a remarkable and basic fact came to light. It was discovered that the numerous visitors breathed out moisture inside the building of which about 15 tons was absorbed by the stonework only to be given off again during the winter. As a result the humidity levels inside the building, so vital to the well being of the painting which is on wood, remain within safe tolerances. So because of those who come to look, wonder and admire, both painting and building are able to co-exist in harmony.

But what is it which draws so many people to Cambridge and to King's Chapel, and why has the building been described as unique and unlike anything else in the world? The answers must remain as varied as are the reactions of those visiting the Chapel but certain well defined points of agreement do stand out. Many, for example, find it impossible to stand in the centre of the ante chapel looking up at the perfect proportions of the building and its soaring fan vaulted roof without accepting that the hand of man must surely have received divine inspiration at the time it was built.

Undoubtedly King's College Chapel has a peculiar power over the mind of man but it is sometimes difficult for him to decide just what it is. A poet will react in one way, the architect in another. Thus we have Wordsworth's famous sonnet which tells us:

> *"that branching roof*
> *Self-poised, and scooped into ten thousand cells,*
> *Where light and shade repose, where music dwells*
> *Lingering—and wandering on as loth to die;*
> *Like thoughts whose very sweetness yieldeth proof*
> *That they were born for immortality."*

The Rev. Augustus Austen Leigh, a former Provost of the College, was able to express the essential qualities of the building in a more tangible way. "It is," he said, "a cathedral in size but a college chapel in plan." He also drew attention to one of the most remarkable factors of the building—its apparent unity of design. Important modifications were introduced during the seventy years or so that the Chapel was under construction and yet the whole appears as the creation of a single night. In this it is unlike so many English cathedrals which derive much of their charm from the amalgamation of architectural styles of different periods.

Only perhaps, at York Minster can one find the same effects produced by a long stone vault combined with an equally long line of rich glass; although at York they are not brought into such close contact with each other. King's College Chapel produces an impression which is both instantaneous and permanent. It does not disarm criticism but it compels admiration. Austen Leigh suggests two ways in which the visitor can test such a proposition for himself; "If anyone is inclined to criticise, let him look at the exterior on a moonlight night from the south side of the quadrangle or from the top of Trinity Street; or let him take his stand within the ante chapel at the north west corner on a bright summer's day, and cast his eye along the coloured glass and stone vaulting till he catches a part of the east window rising above the stately rood-loft; and if he does not feel that there is an inspiration in the building which is above criticism, he must be a 'Man that hath no music in himself.' "

It is true to say that Henry VI succeeded in dominating Cambridge in more ways than one when he set out the specification for his Chapel in his famous "Will". Of his grand design for the complete College only the Chapel was completed yet it is tall enough to impress itself upon the Cambridge skyline and is easily recognised from Madingley hill to the west and the Gog Magog hills to the east. The four spires and intermediate battlements of the building, which have been likened to the legs and teats of an old sow on her back, can be seen from many parts of the University and City. The standards set by Henry and his men still tend to overawe planners and architects more than 500 years later, particularly those concerned with the growth of Cambridge in the years following the Second World War.

All new projects are considered against the skyline which was moulded by the craftsmen and designers of Henry's day. Such is the insistence that whatever is done must be exactly right that the City tends not to build at all. What a contrast to the specification, design and construction which the Chapel's builders undertook with such panache. It is unlikely that a building will ever appear in Cambridge which will challenge the glory of King's College Chapel, but that is no excuse for not trying.

Kings College Chapel

Chapter One

K ING'S College Chapel has for so long been the major landmark on the Cambridge skyline that it is difficult to envisage a time when Cambridge was without it. But there was a time when Milne Street passed through the site of the chapel from north to south at a point where the south door now stands. Piron Lane ran in east-west direction parallel with what is now the southern wall of the chapel. Other streets criss-crossed the site before Henry VI, the founder, commenced to build upon it.

Henry was less than 19 years of age when in 1440 he began the foundation of his college at Cambridge. Three years later the connection between the new college at Cambridge and that at Eton on the Thames was established and the link has remained both strong and continuous to the present day. Henry's aim in founding King's College was "To extirpate heresies, to increase the number of clergy and to provide ministers of religion whose life and doctrine would give light to his subjects."

Originally the college was to consist of a Rector and twelve scholars and it was to bear the name St Nicholas on whose day, 6th December, Henry was born. The choice of the site was left to three Commissioners and it is not difficult to imagine these three gentlemen prowling the narrow dock streets of riverside Cambridge rejoicing in the fact that the King's authority was with them and that they only had to raise their little fingers to cause a lot of people considerable inconvenience.

At that time some old buildings of Clare Hall* abutted onto the west side of Milne Street. The southern end of this street remains and is now known as Queens Lane, but in the fifteenth century it continued northwards until it reached Michael House, the buildings of which then occupied the south west corner of what is now the Great Court of Trinity College. Our three Commissioners no doubt walked around this area for some time and eventually acquired part of a garden belonging to Trinity Hall and this provided the area for the College which Henry contemplated.

Henry laid the first stone of his new college on 22nd April, 1441 and granted the use of materials from the old Norman Castle which overlooked the river at Castle Hill. His first chapel was of modest size and remained on the south quadrangle for about 100 years. Its exact position would have been a short distance to the north of the present chapel and it seems to have been both temporary and uncomfortable. Dr Caius† called it "a mean and inconvenient building" and it duly collapsed in 1536. No trace of it now remains.

The establishment of the link with Eton brought about a change in the status of Henry's new college at Cambridge. It was now called the College of The Virgin Mary and St Nicholas and in its new form was to consist of a Provost, 70 Fellows or scholars, together with a body of chaplains, lay clerks and choristers. William Millington ex-

---

*Founded in 1326 as University Hall and refounded by Lady Elizabeth de Clare as Clare Hall in 1338.
†In 1348 Edmund Gonville founded a College which was re-founded in 1557 by Dr. Caius. Although today more accurately Gonville and Caius it is more commonly called Caius College. Caius being pronounced "Keys".

 Reproduction in black and white of a painting of King's College Chapel by Joyce Conway Evans.

changed the title of Rector for that of Provost, and Provost is what the head of the College is called today. Eton scholars were to be transferred to the College "when sufficiently imbued with the rudiments of grammar."

Surprisingly for one so young, Henry had succeeded in arriving at a grand design for the buildings but, as events subsequently unfolded, the present Chapel was the only part of his visionary scheme to be completed. He took as his model for the Chapel William of Wykeham's two colleges at Winchester and Oxford and in a document known as his will dated 12 March, 1448, gave complete details for his final plan for the Chapel, the southern quadrangle and the western cloister which he intended to build at a later date. Even though the Chapel was the only building to be constructed it follows his Will with surprising accuracy. Civil war and changes in the monarchy delayed completion of the fabric for over half a century but the modifications which occurred in design are only detectable to the eye of an architect.

Henry laid the first stone of the present Chapel on St James Day, 25th July, 1446 and he granted to the college a quarry at Thefdale near Tadcaster which had already supplied material for a large part of York Minster. Two or three years later another quarry of Yorkshire limestone at Huddleston was also given to the college and the material was no doubt brought to the site by water. An interesting sidelight to the use of stone on King's College Chapel is readily visible to anyone who cares to stand on the far side of the Great Court and take a distant look at the south face of the building. The white magnesian limestone from Yorkshire, used throughout most of Henry's reign, is easily distinguishable from the ocolitic limestones from Northamptonshire

A person named Best spent some time inside the north west tower in 1776 to leave his imprint.

Rodney Tibbs

One of the original builders left his personal mark in the roof and then signed it. From this we know that three interlocked diamonds stood for Richard Morris. Rodney Tibbs

and Rutland with which the Chapel was eventually completed. A line of demarcation between the two materials runs from low down at the western end upwards at about 45 degrees to finish high on the eastern extremity.*

Of course it would be pleasant to play detective and try to establish just how far the building had progressed before Henry died in 1471. Unfortunately this is not possible, for Northamptonshire stone from King's Cliffe was supplied under an agreement reached in 1460 and it is possible that some of this building material had been used before the King's death.

The Master Mason, Reginald Ely, appears to have been the man responsible for much of the early design of the Chapel. He would probably have taken as his model the Lady Chapel at Ely Cathedral, but in 1476 John Woolrich succeeded to the position

*See photograph on Page 56.

KING'S COLLEGE

Miscellaneous Selection of Masons' Marks in the Chapel and on the Gatehouse to the Old Court

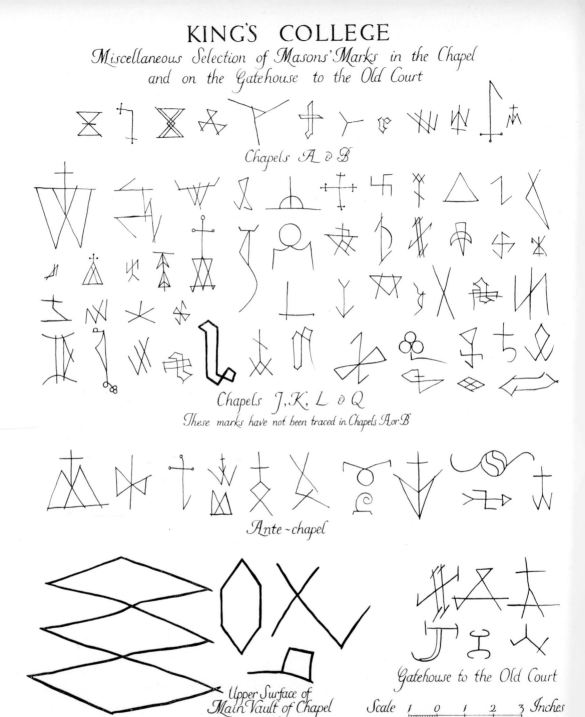

Chapels A & B

Chapels J, K, L & Q
These marks have not been traced in Chapels A or B

Ante-chapel

Upper Surface of Main Vault of Chapel

Gatehouse to the Old Court

Scale 1 0 1 2 3 Inches

Reproduced by kind permission of the Royal Commission on Historical Monuments—Crown Copyright of Master Mason and the vaulting shafts which he placed in the choir, and which spring from corbels at the transom level show that he had decided to adopt what was then the new fashion of fan vaulting. In fact the vault itself was built by other workers 30 years later. These days it is almost impossible to think of the Chapel as an unfinished pile of building work which stagnated for lack of interest and money, but such was the case immediately after the death of Richard III in 1485. Richard had contributed largely towards work on the chapel but with his passing the College found itself in a parlous financial state and unable to carry on without outside help.

The famous vaulted roof had not yet appeared and it is likely that the interior was closed off from the rain and winds of the Fens by a wooden covering. There is evidence to show that a temprorary wall at the western end sealed off the five eastern bays and that a temporary south doorway was built through the fourth southern side chapel from the east. Understandably there followed, for over 20 years, a period of complete hiatus. The Wars of the Roses raged and kings seemed to gain and lose the throne with monotonous regularity*. Although Richard III had been, rather surprisingly, a

---

*1455, first battle of Wars of the Roses fought at St Albans. Henry VI, having been defeated, lost the throne to Edward IV but regained it in 1469 when Edward fled to Flanders. He lost it again in 1471, was imprisoned and died the same year.

Above the fan vault but below the roof is this enormous space where a man may walk. The steel tie rods were added during roof work in 1860 by Sir Giles Scott.

Royal Commission on Historical Monuments—Crown Copyright

generous patron it was not until Henry VII took an interest in the College just before his death that matters began to move again.

After a reminder from the college that his great-uncle's work stood abandoned he saw for himself the true situation when he visited Cambridge in 1506 to celebrate St. George's Day at the College. In the summer of 1508 more than a hundred men were again at work and only three weeks before his death, in the following year, Henry conveyed the sum of £5,000 to the College and asked his executors to provide as much further financial support as might be necessary to finish the job. During 1515 the fabric of the chapel was finished. John Wastell of Bury St Edmunds was the last Master Mason to work on the chapel and to him must go the honour of final completion.

As a young mason Wastell worked on Saffron Walden Church, not so many miles away to the south east and it is believed that he also worked on the beautiful old church at Lavenham, near Sudbury in Suffolk. He signed a contract with Henry Semark to build the now famous great vault and finish it within three years. Although by July 1515 the main fabric of the building was finished at last there is reason to believe that poor Wastell died a month or so earlier and may not have seen the final product.

Anyone who has been involved in a new building project would possibly have some idea of how both the workmen and the members of the College felt, as the end came in sight. Admittedly only the main fabric was complete, the lengthy business of preparing the interior furnishings, adding to the windows, and indeed the floor, was to continue over a further period of years. But there it stood, clean and fresh and with that clear cut value which seems to go with stone before wind and weather begin their inexorable process of steady erosion and weathering.

It must have been a splendid moment and even though, from that day to this men have stood at varying distances and looked at the chapel from different prospects, few can recapture the emotion which must have belonged exclusively to those whose hands had worked upon it. Did they realise they had just completed one of the great buildings of the world? I am certain in my own mind that they did.

The east end of the Chapel before the present scheme and the siting of the "Adoration of the Magi".
Royal Commission on Historical Monuments—Crown Copyright

Chapter Two

VISITORS to the Chapel today are in a most fortunate position, for unlike those thousands of people who have worn away the entrance stones in the intervening years, they can stand inside the building and look at an interior which, in texture and colour, exactly resembles that which the original builders were able to admire.

During the period 1965 to 1968 King's College has spent over £150,000 on the most complete cleaning and restoration programme ever carried out in the long history of the Chapel. The reasons and the problems which caused and had to be faced in this particular undertaking are discussed in greater detail later in the chapter. The immediate result which makes a visit to the building such a memorable experience lies in equal part in clever cleaning of the fabric, sensitive redesign and the achievement of a magnificent setting for Rubens' "Adoration of the Magi", which was bought at a world record price of £275,000 in 1961 by Major A. E. Allnatt and then given to the College.

Even before that time the College was considering the aesthetic and liturgical shortcomings of parts of the interior of the Chapel and the arrival of the painting acted as the catalyst for a considerable amount of related thought and activity. So successful has been the interior cleaning and restoration of the stonework that at least one pair of visitors found themselves disappointed. As they left the Chapel the man turned to his wife and said "Nothing seems to be sacred these days my dear. It is not the same as it was, they have obviously put a completely new roof on it."

Sir Martyn Beckett, the architect chosen by the College to undertake the redesign of the east end of the chapel as a setting for the Rubens and to supervise the restoration work, came to a fundamental decision early on in his scheme which obviously caused the visitor to think the roof was new. At a very early stage in the Chapel's history the walls were protected with a lime wash and this has been cleaned off and replaced at various times during the intervening years. Until now the lime wash has served the valuable purpose of protecting the stonework from the ingress of carbon deposited on the walls by the burning of the numerous candles which normally light the choir stalls and other parts of the building.

An almost completely smokeless candle was located in Scandinavia and subjected to rigorous tests as a result of which it became obvious to Sir Martyn that the traditional lime wash could be dispensed with altogether. The stonework was then thoroughly cleaned and left in its original state. The result is dramatic and in the place of the rather cold texture of limewashed stone we have the gloriously warm and mellow tones of the magnesian limestones which take up a soft honey colour as the sun filters through the famous and priceless stained glass windows of the building.

So much of history occurs by chance and Sir Martyn's account of how the smokeless candle came to be discovered is worth recalling. "My colleague and assistant went to a restaurant in the suburbs of London for dinner with his wife and on the table in the restaurant was a red candle which he noticed was not smoking. He said to the proprietor, 'Where do you get these from?' and was told they were Swedish and that there was a supplier in the East End of London. It was from there that we found out about the candles. It really was a happy accident. We then obtained a consignment for King's from this supplier and analysed them in a Cambridge laboratory. It was found that they were made purely of animal fat and not wax at all. We later put them under test and discovered that the deposit was minute compared with the ordinary wax."

Sir Martyn told me when we discussed this basic turning point in the scheme that the College bursar had visited various churches and buildings in Stockholm which used the smokeless candles and was very impressed with the results. Subsequent scientific tests, carried out by the Building Research Centre on behalf of the College in the Chapel itself, showed that only about one twentieth of the carbon of traditional candles was released into the atmosphere. The present scheme also included the fitting of specially designed electric lighting which would enable the candles to be used only on special occasions, and this caused Sir Martyn to make up his mind about the removal of the lime wash for good. "Not only had we eliminated by twenty times the carbon in the air but had already reached the point where the candles would only

Masons marks cut into the stone in the loft space above the vault not only located the position of each piece but identified the craftsman.   *John Redman*

The plans show, above, the floor design introduced by James Essex in the 1770s and, below,
the 1702 design reinstated by Sir Martyn Beckett.

be used for about one fifth of the time they would previously been alight," Sir Martyn adds, at the same time expressing the hope that interior cleaning will not be necessary again in his lifetime.

The elimination of unnecessary carbon and candle grease from the atmosphere of the Chapel was important from the point of view of the valuable painting which had now found a permanent home in the building. When one remembers that the Chapel was previously cleaned shortly after the Second World War and that in a comparatively short space of time it had become thoroughly grimy the outlook, at such a rate of deterioration, would not have been too happy for the surface of the painting.

In all the moves which followed, the provision of a suitable setting and environment for the Rubens took a high priority in the mind of both the architect and the College committee which collectively took decisions as the work went along. Main-

One bay, cleaned as an experiment, contrasted strongly with the grime covered interior that remained.
Edward Leigh, Cambridge.

taining the correct humidity from this aspect immediately dictated the type of heating to be installed, for, apart from their unsightliness and inefficiency, the old wall radiators which were fitted to the Chapel produced heavy convection staining on the walls. It took Mr. David Russell of Rosser and Russell, the heating consultants called in on the problem, exactly 30 minutes to make up his mind that underfloor heating was the only suitable method of heating the Chapel because of its cubic content, shape and section. It was also the most suitable for the preservation of the Rubens.

As the planning of the restoration programme went along it was becoming obvious that the final solution to any one problem was to be found in an immense jigsaw puzzle in which the pieces, although difficult, were undoubtedly right once they had been fitted together. The type of candle suggested the wall cleaning treatment and finish and this in turn made demands upon the heating system. But once underfloor heating had been decided upon attention naturally turned to the problem of the floor.

Sir Martyn had already made up his mind that there were aesthetic problems which awaited an answer in the floor, for the 1702 design on part of the floor gave way to a fussier and more delicate design in the choir, which had been introduced by the Architect, James Essex, in the seventeen-seventies. As soon as the position of the painting was fixed at the east end the need for alterations of floor levels became clear and the reinstatement of the original floor pattern was considered highly desirable. There was a stage when the College thought in terms of floor heating for the west end only, terminating the work at the organ screen but the experts pointed out that this would only be nibbling at the problem and that other undesirable effects and difficulties could arise from a partial system.

To completely remove and relay the floor was a rather daunting prospect which carried with it some rather nice problems. Striking a correct level, for example, needed careful thought. At the west end the depth to which the contractors could excavate was limited by the presence of vaults about five feet from floor to ceiling and covered by small tudor brickwork arches. Once a sufficient number of inches had been allowed for the underfloor heating and the replacement of the marble floor slabs there was the height of the altar and its relationship to the painting at the far end to be borne in mind. Sir Martyn's scheme aimed to get the top edge of the picture below the bottom of the stained glass window at the east end when viewed from all normal distances and this meant that altar and floor levels left very little room for manouevre. In the event all worked out satisfactorily but there were times, once work on floor removal had begun, when it seemed to those engaged on the task that the difficulties might not melt away so easily.

The College committee, Sir Martyn, and a number of experts and advisors involved in the project continued to meet regularly and gradually the Chapel interior which presents itself today was determined. The next step was to make some preliminary alterations in the chapel to see how the proposals would look in practice and in due

One of the Rattee and Kett craftsmen who was responsible for the repair of many of the heraldic beasts. This Griffon is a modern work not intended for the Chapel but it does illustrate the mason's age old dictum, "one false move can spoil the lot".   *Rodney Tibbs*

course the Edwardian wooden panelling by Detmar Blow was removed from the east end, the picture was placed in position and a small exhibition of drawings and models was staged in one of the ante-chapels to test reaction.

Sir Martyn had mixed feelings about this stage of the proceedings and described his misgivings to me with characteristic good humour. "It was decided to at least move the picture from where it was on an easel in the ante chapel and put it at the right level in relation to the window at the east end to see how it would look, without altering the levels of the floor. The result was that it was very low down on the floor. There were five steps up and there was a sort of sawn off altar. It looked rather dotty and I knew it would and I was a bit upset by that because I thought it would look so dotty that nobody could possibly visualise it as it would eventually be with the levels altered."

And for a while the great and imposing mass of King's Chapel gazed down on the dottiness of it all and visitors came and went. Members of the College inspected the temporary layout, which incorporated some rather elaborate candelabra with ingenious lighting control systems in them, and then went and peered through the clever scale models which the architect had created. They looked at the sightlines, studied the proposed floor pattern and began the interminable argument about the interplay of colour on the Rubens and in the window of the east end.

But in due course the College committee met again. Sir Martyn's scheme was accepted and he was commissioned to proceed with the work as soon as possible. Rattee and Kett, the Cambridge firm, have for years looked after the chapel fabric became the main contractors for the restoration. With their experience on St Pauls, the Houses of Parliament and a number of important buildings up and down the country their craftsmen looked forward to yet another period of activity on this famous building at their doorstep.

". . . .funny old chaps with rugged features with beards, and moustaches and mutton chop whiskers,. . . ."
Ramsey and Muspratt, Cambridge

Chapter Three

TO VISIT King's College Chapel is a memorable experience which is never forgotten and the lengths to which some people will go to make a visit is extraordinary. I was told of the American lady and gentleman, conspicuous by their Stetson hats and festoons of cameras, who got into conversation with the Chapel staff one day. They explained that they had flown over from the United States simply to visit two English buildings, Coventry Cathedral and King's College Chapel, Cambridge.

They gazed at King's lofty vault and said of the two buildings "There is no comparison is there?" Unfortunately they did not indicate which, in their view, did not compare with the other but from their manner one could make a reasonable guess. They then left for London airport well pleased with their two-day jaunt across the Atlantic.

One normally enters the Chapel through the south west door to find oneself magically transported away from the noise, pressures and bustle of the twentieth century. There is that faint but all pervading whisper which seems to go with large buildings and even if the day is dull outside the superb stained glass windows shed a soft, warm glow across the marbled floor and the massive wooden organ screen which divides the interior of the Chapel into two halves.

If one walks to the centre of the western end, or ante chapel as it is known, and turns to look east Rubens enormous work of art is seem framed by the organ screen arch. The effect is strangely compulsive and beckoning and, as one approaches the painting and the altar in front, the redesigned east end of the Chapel comes into view. It is uncluttered, the clean stone walls making a simple, some say stark, setting for the richly ornamented altar cloth, the velvet tones of the painting and the famous east window.

But it was not like that when Sir Martyn first began to consider how best the "Adoration of the Magi" could be housed and displayed. At that time extensive wooden panelling by Detmar Blow obscured the walls at the east end and blended into the woodwork of the choir stalls which still remain. Three statues by J. R. Skeaping, R.A., stood in niches in the panelling and the mood was sombre, almost oppressive.* Each generation, it seems, reflects itself in the building, for the schemes which have been drawn up in the past are numerous and fortunately only a few have ever been put into effect. The Victorians, for example, envisaged an east end liberally coated in that peculiar tobacco stained marble of which they were so fond but mercifully this did not come about.

Before Sir Martyn came on the scene another firm of architects, Maguire and Murray, had already been asked to propose a scheme. This they did but it was not

---

*If these were to be displaced, the College was concerned to find a worthy setting for them elsewhere. They are now seen to great advantage in Lincoln Cathedral, in the ambulatory behind the Sanctuary.

 The author with an early winch accidentally left in the north gallery under the roof. It is believed to date from the re-leading of the roof in 1860.

John Redman

"Conceived of as a unit. . . .''. This unusual close-up of the roof was taken from the special scaffolding.

Ramsey and Muspratt, Cambridge

acceptable to the College Committee. The firm were specialists in church architecture and have been responsible for some splendid schemes, many in modern churches. They subscribed to an idea which would have placed the altar in the centre of the main aisle, a sort of "church in the round" if one can borrow from stage terminology, and, as one might expect, the suggestion was given a mixed reception from the College.

Many members were quick to point out that King's Chapel could scarcely be viewed in terms of 'Church in the round' when the building was renowned for its elongated rectangular plan. But it was at this point that the suggestion to remove the wooden panelling from the east end originated and this was carried over into the later schemes.

Another feature of the early and very careful consideration which was given to future Chapel layout and the position of the Rubens was an approach by the College to several eminent men, well versed in art and its history. They were asked to give their opinions as to where the painting ought to be displayed, for at this early juncture it was by no means a foregone conclusion that it would be placed at the east end. Among the experts were Sir Anthony Blunt, Director of the Courtauld Institute and Surveyor of the Queen's Pictures, from Oxford, Sir Kenneth Clark, sometime Director of the National Gallery, Sir John Summerson of the Soane Museum, a distinguished architectural writer, and Professor Nicholas Pevsner, another architectural authority of repute. As in so many distinguished bodies of the past the four individuals duly presented their reports as to where each thought the painting should go, but there was no unanimity in their proposals. Controversy, therefore, emerged early in the deliberations on the Chapel and of course it has persisted ever since. But controversy is usually a direct measure of respect and affection, for few people bother to argue and discuss that which fails to interest them. King's Chapel will merit discussion for as long as it stands and history will surely show that our own century was not an exception.

Re-pointing the open joints in a fan vaulted ceiling boss. Each boss is carved from a solid piece of stone.
Edward Leigh, Cambridge

Sir Martyn recalls that when he originally approached the problem of the picture and its position the final solution was by no means obvious. He played around with several ideas and his first scheme positioned the painting some twenty-five feet out from the end wall and provided it with something of an island setting.

"When I saw it there, and having regard to sight lines and other things, I revised my opinion. Obviously it depended where you were in the Chapel, but the top of the picture did tend to cut into the bottom of the east end window."

So the painting went back closer to the wall, leaving the top some distance from the bottom of the mediaeval glass of the east end. At this stage the discussion about conflict of colour tone and quality between the opacity of the painting and the transluscence of the glass began to emerge but Sir Martyn was not so bothered by this as some people and I think his explanation is worth setting down for the record.

"I never thought it was as great a problem as some people seemed to think, because I have always believed that our eyesight has got its own angle of vision and you cannot, because of physical reasons, look at the window and the picture at the same time. Once you are through the organ screen you are either looking at the picture or you are looking at the window and it seemed, to me at least, that you are not taking in the window and the picture at the same time.

"What bothered me more was the fact that it was a Flemish baroque picture in a perpendicular gothic chapel; this does not matter in most churches or cathedrals because they are all of different dates and have been built and added onto over hundreds of years, therefore having different objects of different dates is immaterial, but this is all of one piece and this is what bothered me. The fan vaulting runs from one end to the other and it was all conceived of as one unit.

"I felt that here was a picture of such a different school, date and country that I had to ask myself seriously, how it would look? I always felt that it ought to be the focal point of the east end. It was painted as an altar piece by Rubens for a church in Antwerp and I did not see any reason why it should not be an altar piece in King's really."

Sir Martyn produced many drawings and evolved many treatments showing how the painting ought to be presented at the east end. The very first scheme showed it in a baldachino but as he progressed with the design it began to gain simplicity. First one item of the surround was removed and then a further piece would be taken off until eventually the architect decided that the obvious framework for the picture was the magnificence of King's Chapel itself. Few men, he considered, could improve on that.

"Some people would argue that the finished scheme is too simple, particularly the bare walls, but I think this is what, in fact, makes it so marvellous. The architecture adds to the picture and the picture adds to the architecture, and the whole thing repercusses back and forth."

34

The reaction of a visitor to this particular aspect of the scheme is likely to be decided by his own personal relationship to the Chapel. If he is visiting it for the first time he will react in an uncomplicated way to the scene which is set before him. He may like it, he may not. But one has to remember that to many thousands of people the Chapel is an old friend, a constant source of enjoyment and delight and they may have been calling upon it for over 50 years. I have a feeling that if somebody messes about with the interior when I am an old man I might well resent it.

Equally obvious to the architect in the early stages of preparing his scheme was

A party of visitors give scale to the west towers and masonry. Note the iron spikes to deter night climbing undergraduates and the emblems near the tops of the pinnacles.   *Rodney Tibbs*

John Saltmarsh, the King's historian, points to the nearby tower of St John's College.

the need to do something about the floor design. As the illustrations in this book* show there was a bold yet fluid design in the choir but nearer the altar it was both messy and finicky and completely out of scale with the remainder of the building. So aesthetic considerations dictated the lifting of the floor, heating needs pointed to the same thing, while the need to lower the Rubens and the altar level also pointed to a major upheaval at ground level. Just what was discovered when the floor was removed forms part of the next chapter. To me there is always something thrilling about a literal digging up of the past and in the case of the west end of the Chapel the floor was coming up for the first time since it was laid in 1774. Lifting the floor also gave the architect the opportunity to reinstate the original floor design and this in turn provided the contractors with an interesting hunt for the raw marble which would exactly match the magnificent black and white squares of the original. The basic design was not too difficult to work out but, Sir Martyn said afterwards, it did mean days at the drawing board playing a form of chess on the grand scale with squares of black and white.

Gradually the needs of the Chapel and the finest combination of technical and aesthetic skills to shape it for the next generation or so began to fit into place. To determine what course one is going to take with such a building requires immense self confidence and ability. One is aware of following on behind artists and craftsmen of the highest skills, and of making alterations directly affecting a piece of fabric which is finely knitted into the very historical background of England.

I always feel that because of its sense of unity and the excellence of documentation —Henry's Will for example—it is easy to get close to the men who were responsible for the construction. One is not dealing with an edifice which has been constantly added to or modified by different generations and therefore impersonal to a degree' but one man's concept clearly stated, set out and constructed by a small group of superb craftsmen.

Even the mechanics of their building are worthy of today's study. They not only hoisted considerable tonnage of stone into the air, they kept it there, and with such artistic skill that the mass seems to float on a few fine columns of stone. There is an old story, certainly repeated by Horace Walpole, that Sir Christopher Wren himself would go and gaze at the great vault and say that he would undertake to build just such another if any man would tell him where to set the first stone.

Against this rather awe-inspiring background the College and their advisers set out on the journey of restoration. There were many unknown factors and it was obvious that some very special techniques would have to be worked out and developed as the task proceeded. But the broad plan of action existed and everyone working on the project knew what the ultimate objects would be. All that remained was to establish methods which would do justice to the Chapel and which would justify the work carried out in the eyes of the generations to come.

*See pages 24 and 25.

The south face. Lighter stone at the bottom of the towers marks, to this day, the point reached at this end of the building when construction ceased for 15 years in 1461. *Rodney Tibbs*

Chapter Four

BEFORE any restoration work could begin on the Chapel a tremendous amount of protective work had to be undertaken and a suitable system of scaffolding evolved. For the lower part of the building a special casing of hardboard was constructed up to the level of the bottoms of the great windows. In this way the delicate detail of the magnificent carved heraldic beasts, the Royal Arms for England of Henry the Seventh, the heraldic greyhounds and dragons, the crowns, the fleurs de lys and other delicate work was protected from the coming and going and the manouevring of poles and steel.

Mr. R. Hardwick of Messrs Rattee and Kett, the man primarily responsible for deciding exactly how the whole massive programme should be carried out and integrated, told me that he had the idea of proceeding along the full length of the chapel, bay by bay with a specially constructed gantry made of scaffolding. The details and the exact lengths of the necessary poles were worked out in advance and the gantry was made outside the Chapel. It was then dismantled and moved inside the building and built in three sections to cover three bays. Whilst work proceeded on the second and third bays the scaffolding from the first and rearmost bay was dismantled and then rebuilt in front of the third section and in this way the entire gantry was moved along the Chapel without hitch or unnecessary delay.

Not only did the system ensure continuity of progress, it made certain that the work went along at a predetermined pace for the entire restoration programme had to be fitted into a limited space of time in order that various Chapel commitments, especially the Christmas Eve broadcast service, could be met.

The gantry enabled the cleaners, the stonemasons, the stained glass experts and all the other craftsmen to restore one complete bay of the Chapel a month and thus with a total of twelve bays the work was calculated to last exactly one year. Because it was shaped to the dome of the roof the gantry enabled workmen to stand at a comfortable arms length from the vaulting at any distance from one side of the forty foot wide building to the other. Cleaning was carried out by means of vacuum machines not unlike the domestic vacuum cleaner, washing with water only and brushing with a variety of bronze brushes.

Even though the amount of water used on the building was carefully regulated it was obvious at an early stage that tremendous quantities would be used as the work went along, and if work was not to be held up unduly the gantry would have to embody its own plumbing system. It was uneconomic that the men engaged upon the cleaning work should have to haul water up and down the scaffolding and so a system of water tanks was designed and incorporated into the structure. Fresh water was taken from

The east end with the Detmar Blow panelling removed and work on lowering the floor level just beginning.

Edward Leigh, Cambridge

the mains and fed into a storage tank on the gantry. The water level was controlled by a simple float valve. Dirty water was emptied into a further tank and discharged through a system of pipes into the drains outside the chapel.

There remained a possible snag. King's Chapel is 80 feet high and Cambridge stands in relatively flat countryside. Would there be enough pressure on the public water mains to lift the water up to the top of the building? Fortunately there was and the complete system worked to perfection.

Much of the grime which coated the interior of the building was found to be carbon surrounded by candle wax. This rested lightly on the previously limewashed surface and much to everyone's surprise a considerable amount of filth could be taken off the stonework by the use of heavy duty industrial vacuum cleaners. This was followed up by careful cleaning by water and brushes and in this way the remaining deposit and the wash which had incorporated three tons of lime when it was applied just after the war, were removed leaving the natural stone.

Mr. Hardwick is of the opinion that the limewash had protected the surface and prevented the carbon from entering the pores of the stone. He remained sceptical and a little worried about the decision to omit the limewash on this occasion because he was unable to believe that any candle was completely free from carbon. He told me, when I discussed the problem with him afterwards, that it was not until he was shown a photograph of a small niche or alcove in which a smokeless candle had burned for many years and he noted a complete absence of blackening of the stonework above that

Tudor brickwork beneath the floor was found to rest directly on the earth below.

Edward Leigh, Cambridge

he admitted to himself that the new candles would work. Normally a candle burning under such circumstances would create a circle of carbon on the ceiling above in a very short space of time.

One of the most difficult problems facing the restoration workers was the protection of the magnificent organ screen. Constructed entirely of wood, the problem was not simply that of excluding dust and guarding against the possibility of damage but of maintaining suitable temperatures and humidities within the protecting material. It was decided to shroud the organ and screen in a hardboard casing with suitable insulating material but the problem of temperatures and humidity looked as though it would be very expensive to overcome when architect and College committee first began looking at the situation.

A figure in the region of £800 was quoted at one stage for equipment to do the job and at this sum all concerned blanched a little. Eventually the inventive Mr. Hardwick put forward an idea which was very cheap indeed and one which was to prove entirely effective. Electric fan heaters were installed inside the protective casing and controlled by suitable thermostats. For as long as the work progressed on the Chapel the air was kept circulating and, when necessary, heated air was passed through the casing. Hygrometers gave constant readings of the state of the atmosphere inside the casing. The Rubens was then moved and enclosed in a box in the area of the screen.

Afterwards when the restoration of the Chapel was complete and the time came to remove the casing it was found necessary to revive the wood and to give it added depth and lustre. A mixture of pure beeswax and turpentine was sprayed on the screen —about 30 gallons in all—and later the screen was left alone before receiving a final rub over and polish. Then came some heartstopping moments. At the stage when wood treated this way normally dries off to the point where it can be polished, the organ screen refused to perform accordingly. Obviously the water used in the cleaning of the stonework was still evaporating into the atmosphere and it was the high humidity which was preventing the wood from going "off", as the carpenters and joiners would say.

But one Monday morning when the workers returned to the building and despairingly gave the screen a rub it began to gleam with a deep lustre. The magic had worked and in no time at all the mouldings and carvings were beginning to look even more splendid than ever.

One of the country's foremost authorities on the restoration of stained glass, Mr. Dennis King, personally supervised the cleaning and restoration of the thirteen thousand square feet of famous stained glass in the magnificent windows. Just how he and his firm set about this monumental task is described in much greater detail in the chapter on the Chapel windows. One can say that by the time the glass restoration work was finished the windows revealed a beauty of colour, depth and tone which has not

The special scaffolding in position. In the background a plastic curtain protects that part which has been cleaned.   *Edward Leigh, Cambridge*

been seen for many many years. Those who worked on the windows, like everyone who had a hand in the restoration and cleaning of the building, had to make use of the gantry whilst it was in position in each bay of the Chapel. In this way the interior appearance of the building was brought to a higher standard than that achieved for many centuries and possibly since the original construction. Both stone and glass, forming a most superlative partnership within the Chapel, were restored to their rightful texture.

As the gantry system was moved along the work which had been cleaned was protected from dust by an enormous polythene curtain which sealed off the back of the system. Once the work on the upper structure had been completed attention could be turned to the lower levels. It was noticed that the heraldic beasts, which mark that part of the Chapel built by Henry VII, had become chipped and damaged throughout the ages and it was suggested to the college that a further one thousand pounds should be spent to set them in order.

This was duly agreed, but a problem arose almost immediately. Unlike the remainder of the Chapel which is built in limestones from Yorkshire and Northamptonshire, the heraldic beasts, portcullises, roses and other intricate decoration were cut in Caen stone. Rattee and Kett's stonemasons nodded approvingly to themselves when they identified the material, for stone from this part of France is recognised as being among the finest materials for delicate carving. Fortunately it was remembered that some enormous blocks of this stone had lain in the stonemasons' yard of the firm for many years, a left-over from a job of the past.

The Caen stone was duly searched for, cut into suitable sized pieces and the work of repair was begun. Odd ears, bits of tails, pieces of formal design, rose petals were carefully shaped out and fitted to the chapel fabric where needed. These days stonemasons have the tremendous advantage over their predecessors in the availability of epoxy resin adhesives. A dragon's tail, for example, can be mounted in position using a bronze dowel drilled into the two adjoining faces and held in place by resin adhesives

Raw material—some of the stone at Rattee and Kett's Cambridge yard which was used to repair the Chapel interior. *Rodney Tibbs*

To enable mediaeval masons and cleaners to get at the interior these rope holes were left, at intervals, through the vaulted ceiling.

John Redman

specially developed for stonework repair. The result is a joint as strong as the original piece of solid stone and very nearly imperceptible at the point where the repair occurs.

Much of the decorative stonework inside the Chapel is superbly detailed, much more so than anyone had realised until the scaffolding was in place and a close inspection was made possible. Binoculars are a useful asset when studying the building from the outside but they can also bring much pleasure if they are used inside the building when the light is suitable. Unfortunately, without them it is impossible to appreciate the full quality of some of the finer work which occurs about twenty feet or so above floor level.

But to return to the restoration. When the walls and windows were complete there remained one of the most daunting tasks of all, that of the removal of the floor.

It was the first time that much of it had been lifted since it was originally laid, at the beginning of the 18th century, and so the operation carried with it an unusual degree of excitement. I have always marvelled at the manner in which mediaeval builders were able to achieve such incredible stability in structures of tremendous tonnage, and King's is no exception. The foundations are of clunch, a sort of compressed chalk, and it turned out that much of the floor, especially the raised portions near the altar, were built straight down onto the mud of the ground beneath by means of tiny arches of brickwork. Slabs of stone were laid across the arches, filling material laid on top of that and finally the floor slabs were placed in position.

The stone slabs found beneath the floor at the east end may have come from an earlier path, for want of a better description, which ran from the Western door to the organ screen. Coles description of the floor in 1742 gives us the clue. "You ascend 2 Steps in Ye Anti-Chapel to come up to Ye Door of the Choir Wch is entirely paved very beautifully from these Steps quite to Ye screen of Ye Altar Wth black and white marble squares in a rectangular figure. This was thus paved about 1690; the pavement of Ye Anti-Chapel, Wch is of an English grey marble, being there before; Wch however did not serve to pave it at all; for on both sides below Ye two doors is only laid with brick on each side of a broad stone pavement of Ye breadth of Ye great W. Door, Wch reaches from that to Ye rest of Ye old part Wch came out of Ye Choir."

Was it part of the "broad stone pavement" which was found under the floor when it was lifted? In my view it is highly likely for they were York stone slabs of about the size which Cole seems to be describing.

Whilst the floor was up the opportunity was also taken to lay hundreds of yards of copper pipe through which hot water now flows to provide the underfloor heating. Mr David Russell of Rosser and Russell, the firm who designed and installed the heating, observed, when he was first called in on the problem, that when the Chapel was built the standard approach to heating was by the design of ecclesiastical vestments rather than by warming the building! But this was not the first time that a heating system had been installed. A rather inefficient system was put in shortly after the first world war which consisted of heating pipes, run in trenches in the ante chapel, also radiators, again mostly in the ante chapel.

The heating it provided was very uneven and, as one might have expected, most of the available warmth was at the ante chapel end leaving the choir to wriggle their toes and shiver under the cassocks on a cold winter's day. Of course the radiators themselves, ornate monstrosities in cast iron, did little to enhance the appearance of Henry's masterpiece and by casting sooty stains up the walls the radiators added considerably to their total absence of charm. It was while humidity tests were being carried out in connection with the Rubens that the remarkable discovery was made concerning the absorbtion by the building of about fifteen tons of moisture breathed out by visitors during the summer. About a third of the moisture is re-evaporated internally

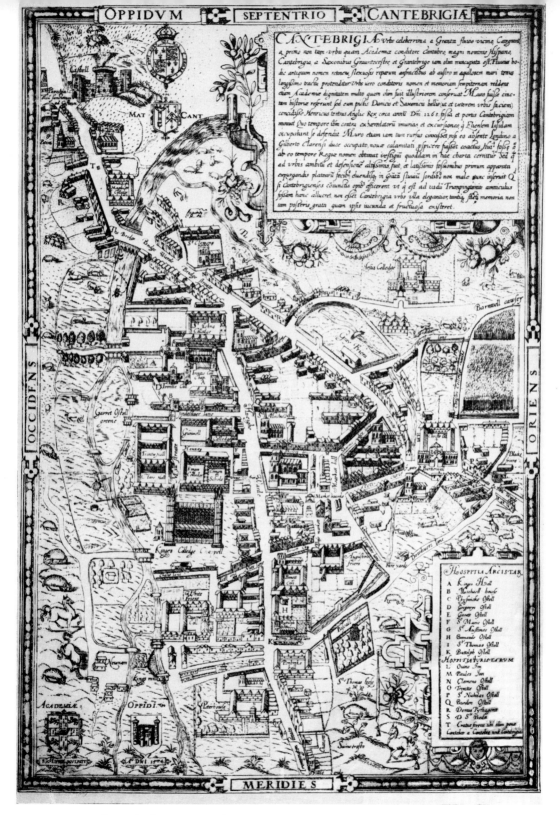

Map by Richard Lyne, 1574, believed to be the first map ever made of Cambridge.
Reproduced by Kind Permission of Cambridge University Library

during the winter and this helps to maintain the relative humidity in the building and prevent the wood on which Rubens painted his "Adoration" from drying out.

It became clear that if the air temperature was not raised too much in cold weather there would not be many humidity problems and it was because of this that a floor heating system was selected as the obvious answer. But there were five considerations which any heating system had to fulfil. Above all it had to be as unobtrusive as possible so as not to detract from the aesthetics of the building in quite the same manner achieved by the first world war design. Further staining of the stonework must be avoided. There had to be a complete absence of noise—the famous service of lessons and carols against a curious background hum or buzz would be unthinkable—and the actual gradient of warmth from floor to ceiling had to be gradual. A lot of hot air in a building eighty feet high would promptly rise and mingle with the fan vaulting leaving the congregation, choir and other occupants to freeze below.

A hot water system and an electric system for heating the Chapel floor were both considered but electricity was rejected on the basis of running cost, greater fluctuations in floor temperature and of course, the inadvisability of tying a long lasting system to one type of fuel. After all it was centuries since the floor had last been lifted and both the college and the contractors hope that an equal space of time will elapse before anyone has to lift the floor again. The fact that a boiler plant of sufficient capacity already existed in the neighbouring Gibbs building made hot water the obvious choice.

For the technically minded may I say that the tubes beneath the floor are of three quarter inch soft copper laid nine inches apart and the water passing through them has a mean maximum temperature of 98 degrees Farenheit, a fraction under blood heat in fact. The tubes are buried about four inches beneath the surface and this means that the temperature of the floor is about 78 to 80 degrees Farenheit in the winter, a level designed to avoid discomfort to the feet. Altogether two and a half miles of copper pipe have been buried in the floor.

The decision to reinstate the floor design of 1702 not only sent Sir Martyn Beckett to his drawing board to play noughts and crosses with black and white squares but it also meant that black and white marble of exactly the right shade and quality had to be obtained from somewhere. Today there are 1,000 black marble slabs in the floor of the chapel and 850 white. It is the proud boast of the craftsmen who worked on the new floor that it would take an expert to tell the new from the old now that they have had some wear. Italy supplied the white marble and Belgium the black.

Both countries went to enormous lengths to locate and supply exactly the material the Chapel needed and both matched each other in the quality of their workmanship. When the marble was delivered it was pre-cut to precisely the right dimensions and so beautifully packed that there was only an occasional breakage. For the white marble the Italian firm reopened an old quarry at Carrar, the only one which contained white marble with exactly the right degree of marking. Fortunately the black marble from Bulge in Belgium was also a highly accurate match. With the floor laid, the walls and windows cleaned and restored, the Rubens painting in position and the earlier panelling by Detmar Blow removed, the chapel neared its final form and style. This chapter has taken a general look at the task and I hope it has conveyed something of the skill of those involved in the workmanship and the courage of those responsible for the design. Other precise details, such as those of the painting and its mount, the restoration of the organ and the problems of the glass I have reserved for those stages at which they fit naturally into our story.

View of the vaulted ceiling showing it; A—before vacuum cleaning; B—after vacuum cleaning; C—the Weldon stone fan vaulting after full cleaning.   *Edward Leigh, Cambridge*

Chapter Five

SEEING THE Chapel and its interior for the first time one may find it is sometimes difficult to orientate oneself to its presence. It is quite possible to wander into the building, to stand staring at its breathtaking vaulted roof and to wander out again as if in a dream and miss many of the most intriguing and important aspects of the building.

In this chapter I have tried to draw attention to one or two of those features of King's which intrigue me and which always make a visit come to life in a manner which is essentially unique to King Henry's masterpiece. One can derive tremendous pleasure and a sense of great purpose and uplift from the building without knowing the first thing about it, but there is much to be said for the alternative approach. I know one man who has had much to do with the fabric and who probably knows the individual stones of the place as well as anybody, and he tells me that he continues to derive more and more satisfaction from the Chapel every time he sets foot in it.

A visit should really begin not at the Chapel but a considerable distance away from it on the south side of the Great Court. From here it is possible to see the entire elevation of the south side of the Chapel and the changes in the colour of the stone to which I briefly referred in an earlier chapter. It was the custom in the days when the Chapel was built to begin at the east end of the building and work upwards and outwards, building in diagonal layers and stepping down towards the west or the left hand side of the building as it is seen from this point. In this way the structure formed a sort of natural staircase for the workmen. The roofless, truncated fragment which Henry VI left behind him can be detected by the change in colour of the stone which runs diagonally across the building from left to right and which continues round the bottom of the building at the south end. The level to which the whiter stone rises marks nearly the limit of the work when it came to a stop in 1461 and in the eastern tower it can be seen rising above the springing of the great window arch. Look at the sides of the buttresses to see the changes in colour best and in the next two buttresses it rises above the second weathering or step in the buttress. From here it progresses steadily downwards until it reaches almost down to ground level on the seventh buttress counting from the eastern end or right hand side.

This part of the chapel, marked for ever in this rather unusual fashion, was all there was of the building when work came to a halt for about 15 years. When it was resumed again in 1476 it went along very slowly until Edward IV began to produce a little more money in 1480. Richard III was also generous and it is believed that by 1485, when Richard died on Bosworth Field, the walls had been taken up to roof level for the distance of the first five buttresses counting from the east.

King's College Chapel. The famous and most photographed view from the footbridge over the River Cam. The Gibbs building to the right contains the boilers which power the Chapel heating system. Clare College buildings are on the left.   *Rodney Tibbs*

These tiny heads were discovered during the cleaning programme. The miniature corbels are each about an inch and a quarter high.
Ramsay and Muspratt, Cambridge

Martin Prentice, the master carpenter at the time, roofed in these five buttresses and filled in the unfinished south end with planking in order to make just under half the length of the building useable for services. There is evidence that a temporary entrance was made through the walls of the fourth side chapel from the east and visitors may check this for themselves by looking below the window of the this side chapel today. They will see a mixture of stones let into the original white magnesian limestone where possibly Simon Clark, the master mason from Bury St Edmunds, broke the temporary entrance through round about 1485. There is an interesting modern counterpart to this theory for not only is there a deep arched recess in the inner chapel wall facing the window but when just after the war some of the panelling in the chapel was taken down for treatment a corresponding arched recess was discovered on the other side also.

If one now walks a little closer to the Chapel by traversing the Great Court on the west side, in other words by walking in front of the Gibbs' building which faces King's Parade, one of the more interesting features of the west end of the Chapel comes into view.

These are the famous Kings Beasts which adorn the four most westerly buttresses and they indicate the influence of Henry VII on the building when he carried on the constructional work in 1500. Henry incorporated considerably more decoration into his section of the Chapel than would have pleased the Founder. Henry VI in his Will asked for it to be "sufficiently boteraced" but instructed that there should not be excessive decoration. His successor, however, had other ideas and the western section built under his jurisdiction shows beasts, heraldic emblems and fine decorative work both inside and out.

Standing outside the Gibbs' building the animals facing us on the buttresses are set in pairs rather as they would be if incorporated on a shield or coat of arms. From left to right, or west to east, they are a lion and antelope, a dragon and greyhound and a further lion and antelope. If one walks round the west end of the Chapel to examine the beasts on the corresponding buttresses we find a lion pairing with a dragon for Henry VIII, a dragon and greyhound for Henry VI and then further dragons, lions and antelopes. By looking at those buttresses which bear this form of decoration one can get a reasonably accurate idea of where Henry VI and Richard III left off and Henry VIII carried on their work.

Whilst walking round the west end of the chapel it is interesting to note the joining line, a few feet off the ground, of the original whiter stone used when the first section of the building was constructed, and the manner in which it gives way to the darker material of the Henry VIII period. The same change of colour can also be seen on the walls of the porch, a few feet above the ground, as we go inside.

The first thing which strikes the visitor to the building when he steps inside is its tremendous height and length. He also becomes aware of the very large areas of glass in relation to stone and the soaring lightness of the vaulted roof which seems to float in the air rather than rest heavily on pillars of stone. Through his construction of the vault Wastell probably earns the description as the greatest of the three architects who worked upon the chapel. It has been described as the supreme achievement of English architecture in any age and, as one stands and gazes up at it, a finer example is difficult to imagine or visualise. It is one of the widest vaults of any kind in the country measuring 40 ft between the piers and 44 ft 6 inches to the glazing in the windows.

It is not only a beautiful and elegant building which Wastell has left us but a fine feat of engineering as well. A mathematician once calculated the weight of the vault at 1,785 tons, or as John Saltmarsh the King's historian, puts it "the weight of a small to medium size merchant ship." The central bosses which punctuate the centre at regular intervals hang down thirty inches from the actual ceiling and are carved from solid stone.

Each "fan" which goes to make up the vault is properly described in architectural terms as "a rectangular portion of a quadrant of an inverted concave parabolic conoid" although I doubt whether many visitors will be able to remember such a splendid mouthful! It is the property of such a conoid that so long as one can prevent the base from spreading it will take a considerable amount of weight without much difficulty. Wastell's mark lies upon the vault of King's and is easily recognised by anyone sufficiently well

One of the newly discovered heads. *Edward Leigh, Cambridge*

versed to look for it. Unlike some designers of vaults he did not attempt to disguise the circular element of the supporting fans, but if anything tended to make a feature of them. In addition to the circular feel of the vaults he succeeded in creating first of all a series of cross arches between each set of fans and, by the clever use of delicate ornamentation, provided also a strong linear motif from east to west along the roof.

It was under Wastell that the west end of the building was constructed for Henry VII and in few places in English Gothic does one come across such an extraordinary display of worldly heraldry. This could have become boring with its endless repetition of the Royal arms for England and Henry VII of the dragon and the greyhound and a series of crowns and fleur-de-lys, crowns and portcullis and crowns and Tudor Rose. But by cleverly altering the style of the greyhounds and dragons Wastell provides us with an entertaining series of animals. Stand in the centre of the ante chapel and look back at the pair over the south door. Here are a formal and very serious pair of animals taking great pride in the coat of arms they are displaying. But to their left in the next bay we find a more naturalistic treatment. The dragon looks as though he really could go on the rampage breathing fire all over the place while the greyhound looks as though the sight of the White City would not give him too much of a shock.

Everywhere there is strong similarity but always minute change. Picking them out can be absorbing and instructive. The use of a pair of field glasses even at such close quarters will reveal precise and exacting detail which is not visible to the normal eye. Indeed it was not until the scaffolding was in position for the cleaning that the delicate detail of much of the running decoration was realised. On some of the pillars, particularly by the north door, are some crocketted pinnacles which are also slightly out of range to the normal eye. Under each pinnacle is a miniature fan vault, also designed by Wastell, and in each vault two little fans at the back are carried on miniature corbels each about an inch and a quarter high. It was on these that tiny faces were found.

John Saltmarsh adds "They are not elegant, handsome countenances like those lovely little angels on the frieze below the windows, these are funny old chaps with rugged features with beards, and moustaches and mutton chop whiskers, in fact just the type of old fellows you might find messing about with trowels, mortar and crowbars. We believe that these were portraits of the principal craftsmen engaged on building the Chapel."*

It was an exciting discovery and one which sets us wishing that the original craftsmen had not been quite so modest. Portraits an inch and a half high so hidden that they might never be found is not in keeping with our own publicity seeking age. I would not suggest that the portraits should have been obtrusive but if they had been accessible from the ground how much greater fun it would have been.

Once the visitor has studied the west end of the Chapel the glimpse of Rubens' painting through the archway of the great wooden organ screen is enough to lure

*See illustrations on pages 29, 52, 54 and 58.

anyone through to the east. Almost too great a lure perhaps because I have noticed numerous people walk straight through the archway without giving it a second look whereas it is certainly one of the major features of the building, apart from the windows.

This extensive and richly wrought wall of wood divides the Chapel into approximate halves and is about ten feet deep. It is through a small door set in the left of the archway that the organist begins his climb to the keyboard of his instrument mounted

South side of Chapel from the Great Court. The change of limestones, referred to on page 17, is clearly shown on the buttresses. *Rodney Tibbs*

on top of the wooden screen but out of sight from ground level. This means that when works involving choir and organ are performed the organist must rely upon an additional conductor placed between himself and the musical director. It all sounds very difficult but I am assured that it works out well in practice.

The organ screen of King's always suggests to me that Henry VIII and Anne Boleyn were, to use a more modern term, rather keen on each other at the time it was constructed. The crowned initials and arms of Henry and Anne suggest a date for the screen somewhere between her coronation in June 1533 and her execution in May 1536 and so for once the short but eventful career of Anne in Henry's household is of considerable assistance to present day historians. Looped initials H.R.A.S. (Henricus Rex, Anna Sponsa) are in the best tradition of a pair of lovers keen to demonstrate their affection for each other in a thoroughly public manner. If one assumes that this demonstrative act occurred at the beginning of Anne's reign rather than a year or so later when she had fallen from favour then a date of 1534 would seem a reasonable guess for this outstanding piece of woodwork.

The choir gates or doors are much younger than the rest of the screen. Here there is no guesswork for they bear the date 1636 and the arms of Charles the First. Somehow they seem positioned in such a manner that they seldom if ever get the attention they really deserve from the visitor. Always he has passed from the west end of the building on his way to the east and he is always anxious to see what lies before him. As soon as he arrives at the choir gates his attention is taken by the Rubens' "Adoration of the Magi" which, with its plain flying side panels, now dominates the altar area.

Rubens painted the "Adoration" in 1634. It is of oils on wood and measures $129\frac{1}{4}$ inches by $97\frac{1}{4}$ inches and was commissioned by the White Sisters of Louvain as an altarpiece. We know that Rubens was paid 920 florins for it before March 9th 1634 and for anyone interested in learning more of his approach to the painting his original sketch is in the Wallace collection in London. The painting was wanted in a hurry and there is a tradition, supported by Sir Joshua Reynolds, that it was completed in eight days. One can say that the painting has a certain freedom of style and expression which amounts to bravura. But even though the painting fetched a world record price when it was bought by Major A. E. Alnatt and given to the college in 1961 it has not always received universal praise.

Reynolds himself called it "a slight performance" but this may have been tinged with professional pique. The attitude in which the Virgin sits has caused some comment. J. B. Descamps observed in his "Voyage Pittoresque de la Flandre" of 1760 that though the painting was "knowledgable and full of finesse" the Virgin did not "sit easily." Again Reynolds says "The Virgin holds the infant but awkwardly, appearing to pinch the thigh." Somehow I do not think the modern visitor will be unduly concerned by these niceties of pose. The spontaneity of the work and the soft glowing lustre of the colours is its chief delight. Rubens himself had a direct connection with Cambridge.

"They are not elegant, handsome countenances. . . ."

Ramsey and Muspratt, Cambridge

During the years 1629 and 1630 he visited London as envoy to Charles the First. He was knighted by the king and given an Honorary M.A. by the University of Cambridge.

The painting itself was formerly the property of the Duke of Westminster and like the rest of the restoration work in the Chapel posed its own problems. It is painted, contrary to the information contained in some books on the subject, on wood and not canvas. Wood is a notoriously fluid material which will move with the slightest change in humidity and temperature and, if this were not sufficient to create difficulties, Rubens chose to use wooden planks which are held together by two vertical battens with the cross members held only by simple metal straps. Whilst the restoration work on the building was in progress the painting was housed in its own specially constructed container which was carefully controlled for temperature and humidity.

But it was when the workmen came to move the painting onto the steel support, specially designed for it by Sir Martyn Beckett, that a nerve straining sequence began. The force exerted by the two lifting winches had to be applied equally on either side of the massive painting, for greater pull on one side would almost certainly have resulted in the wooden planks moving fractionally against each other. Had this happened the College would have found itself possessing a world record price painting with parallel cracks across it from top to bottom. In order to guard against the possibility the contractors chose two of their most experienced men and made them rehearse the pulling action on the winches until they were certain of co-ordinating the force they were applying to the Rubens. Then they carried out the manouevre in earnest and everyone produced an enormous sigh of relief when the painting was safely in its permanent place of rest.

The random size of the blocks of stone beneath this ante-chapel window indicates the point at which a temporary entrance was made. This was during construction when part of the Chapel was sealed off and used for worship. *Rodney Tibbs*

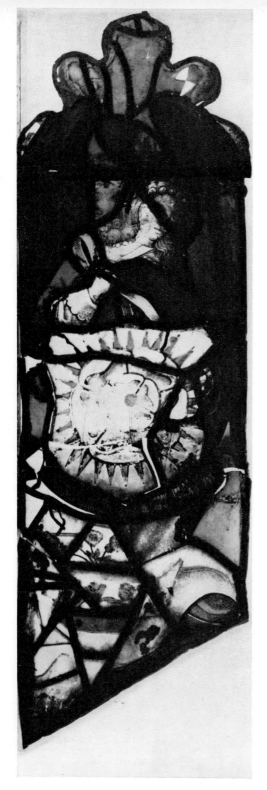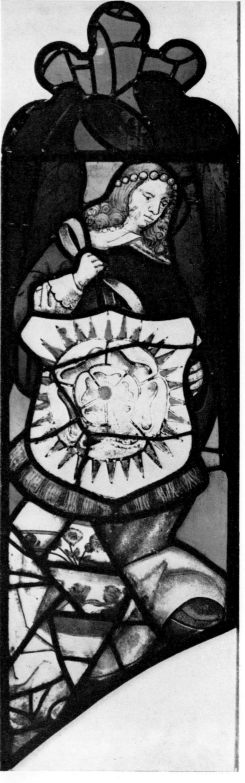

South east window tracery with Tudor rose-en-soleil shield inside out and much broken on left. The same tracery, on right, after restoration.

Chapter Six

ONCE THE decision had been taken by the college to clean and restore the stonework of the chapel it was inevitable that the famous stained glass windows should come in for their share of the attention as well. I am told by Mr Dennis King of Norwich that there is a total of thirteen thousand square feet of glass in the building and he should know, for it was his firm which undertook and carried out the highly skilled restoration and cleaning work which went on from the same scaffolding and gantries as those used by the stone cleaners.

Today the inside of the Chapel positively glows with the myriad tones and colours which go to make up what have been decribed as the largest and most complete series of ancient windows in the world. Today's visitor is again more fortunate than his predecessors of the pre-restoration era for in the process of cleaning and working upon the glass Mr King's men found numerous pieces which were in the wrong way round, others almost opaque with filth and even examples of repairs to the leads which had blotted out considerable detail. I was surprised to learn that stained glass does have a right and a wrong way round until I was shown a piece of mediaeval stained glass at the Norwich workshops. On one side the colour pigment has been burned or fired into the glass leaving plain glass on the other face. In practice the coloured side is mounted on the inside leaving the plain sector to take all the weathering. Nearly all stained glass of an early period shows erosion or pitting on the outer face and in many instances it occurs on the inner face as well. Mr King and his firm have developed their own method of dealing with the outer pitting, a method which they believe is unique. It consists of carefully grinding or abrading away the outer face and carefully repolishing it in order to improve the colour, clarity and light transmission of the glass. Special machines have been designed to do this although considerable skill, knowledge and care is needed on the part of the expert carrying out the operation.

Of course the repolishing method does reduce the thickness of the glass to a point where it can become paper thin. It is then strengthened by the addition of a piece of plain glass, carefully cut to match the shape of the original fragment, and the two bits are sandwiched together when the window pieces are finally re-leaded and the bewildering jigsaw of separate pieces of coloured glass becomes once again a fine stained glass window of a particular pattern or picture design. The technique was originally developed for the restoration of the glass in Winchester cathedral carried out by the same firm but fortunately it did not have to be used too extensively at King's.

Mr King, the name seems highly appropriate, had already cleaned and restored the windows of the westernmost bay, including the great west window in 1967. The following year the task began in earnest and lasted for about as long as the remainder of the work on the fabric, from January to about November. Most of the work involved

One of the ante-chapel panels before restoration.

Rodney Tibbs

brushing the glass and washing it down with plain water. It is not possible to use a detergent for cleaning because it tends to react with the cement which is holding the glass in position in its leading and to soften the adhesive. On occasions, where it is possible to get to both sides of the glass with ease and also use large quantities of clear water to make a thorough job of the washing down process afterwards, mild detergents are used, but this was definitely not the case at King's Chapel.

But in addition to careful washing and brushing with soft brushes a considerable amount of local attention was given by using razor bladed scrapers to remove dirt deposits. Where the condition of the main windows was really poor it became necessary to remove completely the relevant panel and take it away to the Norwich workshops in order that in addition to cleaning it could be completely re-leaded. I watched this operation being carried out by craftsmen with years of experience and they make what must be an incredibly daunting and intricate job look easy. Mediaeval glass, they told me, must always be handled very carefully and the process of restoration begins by taking a rubbing of the entire pane. This produces a jigsaw-like record of the shape of the individual pieces of the panel which is vital to the subsequent rebuilding process. Once the old leading has been removed the window panel consists of no more than a series of scraps of coloured glass and these must go together again later, correct in shape, overall size and every detail.

Horseshoe nails are favoured for pinning the glass and the new lead strip to the craftsman's workbench. These have square tops and sharp points and are ideal for the task. The square top enables the craftsman to press the nail into the bench, using it in thumb tack fashion and, of course, it can always be lightly tapped home with a hammer. I learned that workers in stained glass have to make all their own tools, for the art is practised by so few these days that it is not economic for any commercial toolmaker to produce a line especially for them.

The Norwich firm has been looking after the glass of the Chapel ever since the Second World War and really came into the picture very fully when the choristers' vestry, set in one of the side chapels, was fully reglazed. For this side chapel and other side chapels, for which the reglazing process is still going on, the approach has been to collect stained glass of the period and type appropriate to the chapel and then to incorporate it in the windows. For the benefit of anyone who has not seen the building I should explain that not all the side chapels are fitted with stained glass; although it was originally intended that stained glass be used this was never executed. Some are glazed with plain materials. Dean Ramsey collected a considerable amount of period glass when he was Dean of the Chapel. This, with glass either bought for or given to the College, was put with further glass from Wroxham Hall in Norfolk and built into the choristers' vestry. The main impetus for collecting contemporary glass for this purpose came from Dean Milner-White in the 1920s.

Glass has also been collected in a similar fashion for two windows on the south side which form an extension to the memorial chapel. This elegant little chapel has long commemorated the names of those from the College who died in the First World War. The recent restoration work also added the names of those from the Second World War and refurbished windows and chapel generally.

The fact that experts in stained glass are so few and far between these days provides an incidental benefit as far as buildings of the stature of King's Chapel are concerned. Mr King finds himself called in on glass problems throughout the United Kingdom and so his private collection of glass intended for the King's side-chapels becomes thoroughly representative. I was shown glass from a house in Derbyshire, a fifteenth century roundel and a sixteenth century shield, all of which has been acquired so that construction of a new window could begin. Of course a stained glass window prepared in this fashion is something of a hotch potch of styles but in fairness one must admire the manner in which a skilled eye can bring the material together and provide it with considerable uniformity and beauty. Not all the glass in the side-chapels has travelled vast distances. Some stained glass, deposed by the construction of a fire escape door in the north wall, has simply crossed the width of the building to come to rest on the south side. There was a trip up the road to Norwich for restoration and repair of course.

Historically the windows are very well documented, should anyone wish to learn more of their original construction. Much of their beauty can be attributed to the fact that their dates range from 1515 to 1531, the period when the art of glass painting and firing had really reached a climax. At King's Chapel the earliest glass is that over the north western porch. It was executed by Barnard Flower, a magnificent name I always think. He was a Fleming resident in Southwark and was the first non-Englishman to hold the appointment of King's Glazier, glazier that is to the Monarch of the day, not King's College! When he died in 1517 he had finished, with the help of others, whose names are not known, four windows and all the armorials in the tracery lights.

He was succeeded both as glazier to the King and as constructor of the Chapel windows by Galyon Hone, another Fleming. Hone and three partners, Thomas Reve, Richard Bond, both Englishmen, and James Nicholson, a Fleming, made the famous east window and sixteen others between 1526 and 1531. The remaining four were constructed at the same time by a further Fleming, Francis Williamson and Symond Symondes who was probably English, but under Hone's general instruction. These men lived and worked in England but the style of the glass is essentially that of the best of the Flemish Renaissance. It is almost certain that the designs for many of the later windows were obtained from the famous Antwerp draughtsman and glass painter, Dirick Vellert.

One of the more remarkable things about the glass of the Chapel is the manner in which it has escaped serious damage throughout the years. It is known that the fanatical William Dowsing, who disposed of a considerable amount of church glass on Cromwell's behalf, visited the Chapel on Boxing Day, 1643. His comments on "One thousand Superstitious Pictures" are generally taken to indicate his intention to destroy the glass of the building. Fortunately it survived without any damage during the Civil Wars and there is little trace of defacement by either Puritans or Reformers.

It was thought that Hitler might be the next historical figure to damage the windows and at the onset of the Second World War the glass was removed from the windows and distributed to various parts of the county for safe keeping. Cambridge suffered little war damage and that which did occur did not involve university or other historical buildings. This was attributed by Cambridge people to Hitler's wish to

64

preserve the University for his own use when his victory was complete. For some little time after the war the boarded up windows of the Chapel presented a sombre appearance in King's Parade. Then the glass returned and as the colours glowed once again in the Chapel it seemed to signify that peace and normality was really back again.

The overall scheme of the windows starts from the north-west and represents the "Story of the old lawe and of the new lawe." In most cases the pictures below the central bar of each window illustrate the life of Our Lady to whom the College and Chapel are dedicated, while above the bar is a scene from the Old Testament, the Apocrypha or elsewhere either typical of the scene below or contrasting with it. Even this simple explanation makes the windows a good deal more interesting and under-

A Norwich craftsman re-leads part of one of the famous windows. Note the horseshoe nails used to keep the pieces in position. *Rodney Tibbs*

Careful brushwork was used to remove much of the surface dust from the stained glass.

Rodney Tibbs

standable to the visitor. He might be puzzled by the figures which are in the centre of most of the windows. These are known as 'messengers' and are usually angels or prophets. The scrolls with texts they carry offer an explanation for the pictures on either side of them. They are 94 of these figures, but they are not all different. Seven are used four times, eleven, three times, eight twice and the remaining seventeen once only. Altogether there are 100 huge pictures in the stained glass windows of King's College Chapel*, all of them now fully restored and as clean and crisp to look at as they have ever been.

---

*Details of the Stained Glass Windows are given in Appendix I on page 91.

Chapter Seven

NOT ALL the £150,000 spent on restoration work at the Chapel was devoted to the bricks and mortar. Among the items to receive careful attention was the organ and in this direction the College was able to do something about the aesthetics of the building in addition to its more tangible qualities. Unlike the building the organ does not represent the work of one specific period. Indeed King's has housed a number of organs in its history and the present instrument has the benefit of much which modern technology has brought to organ building.

I think rather than plunge in to the story at the present day or even go back to the very beginning the best introduction to the instrument is to be found in the pages of "Memoirs of a Kings College Chorister" written in 1899 by Thomas Case. This is a rambling work but one which has nevertheless become a minor classic of its type. Case wrote in later life remembering much of his time as a chorister which was set in the Victorian era. Indeed his description of how all the choristers longed for a glimpse of Queen Victoria and Prince Albert when they visited King's Chapel, but found themselves having to bow their heads as the Royal party passed by makes an amusing if slightly pathetic tale.

Recalling a later visit to the Chapel he says "As a most special privilege Dr Mann ("Daddy" Mann, the famous choirmaster and organist) invited me into the organ gallery for the Sunday afternoon service, when, upon reaching the top of the staircase I was taken with surprise by finding myself face to face with the front of the organ, greatly enlarged, having four manuals and 55 speaking stops—to compare with the old keys and stops which I could almost see being fingered sixty and more years ago by Mr. John Pratt, the then organist and choirmaster.

"The bellows handle, which formerly faced the stairs, was a thing of the past, the organ being supplied by wind by new water power machinery placed in the vestry adjoining the one remembered so well, where the choristers, men and boys, assembled previous to going in procession into the choir."

Thus even in the lifetime of Thomas Case the instrument had undergone a considerable amount of change. In this latest restoration, as we shall see later, the organ was to undergo yet more changes designed to modify and improve its tone. But one thing had not altered unduly over the years because it was so well designed when it was constructed. This is the organ case which is the part most obvious to the visitor gazing up at the organ screen and the roof of the chapel. When Thomas Dallam the famous organ maker built the case he took great care to see that it would not unduly obstruct the view of Wastell's already famous roof. It is virtually impossible to improve upon his design in this respect; as the instrument has been modified and modernised over the years the case has remained much as it was. It forms an important feature of the interior of the building and the modern renovators were happy to leave it the way it was.

There is little doubt that the Chapel has always had an organ. The original statutes, drawn up in 1443 insist that of the ten chaplains and sixty lay clerks, one at least should know how to play the organs in the "college church". For the first clear mention of an organ builder we have to come forward to 1508 when Thomas Browne was paid "for making a new great organ." There was certainly an instrument in the building when Queen Elizabeth visited the Chapel in 1564. On that occasion a "Te Deum" was performed "solemnly sung in Prick Song, and the organ playing." A few years later the instrument was removed on the instructions of the Queen's Commissioners and Roger Goad, Provost of the College from 1570 to 1610, behaved in that thoroughly business like manner one associates with King's, and expressed the view that it might just as well be sold as lie idle. This was done, with the result that the Chapel remained organless until 1605-6 when an entirely new instrument was made on the spot by Thomas Dallam. It is the casing of this particular instrument we see today although it is doubtful if any of the original pipes remain.

From a detailed account headed "The Charges About the Organs" we learn that Dallam and his workmen moved from London to Cambridge where they remained from 22nd June 1605 until 7th August 1606. They had lodgings in the town but meals were provided in college. Suppers were provided on Fridays and "fasting nights". Altogether £371 17s 1d was spent of which it has been calculated that £214 can be put down to the organ and £156 to the case. The accounts cover a bewildering range of items and to my mind there is no doubt that the organ builders and their variety of materials must have presented a somewhat bizarre sight as they worked away in the middle of this vast building.

They bought a "grindelstone" and hooked it on a proper frame. They supplied themselves poplar wood in order to make the mandrells upon which the organ pipes were rolled and shaped. Then there was "ebony for the kayes" and a shillingsworth of "flannell clothe to laye under the kayes". The two joiners who made the organ case were Chapman and Hartop and even though they may sound slightly Shakesperean in style they are in no way to be compared with "Knockle the Limber", the man who actually decorated the case with gold and various colours.

Dallam tuned the organ in 1607 and some surplus tin was sold off. Six years later he was back again doing some repairs and there were further repairs in 1617. It was Robert and not Thomas Dallam who repaired it in 1635 and the name Dallam occurs for the last time in 1641 before the organ was taken down to save it from destruction. Another superb name occurs when the instrument was dismantled in 1642-3. He was Magister Genuynge who received £2 for removing the instrument whilst a man called Ashley collected three shillings for taking down the organ case.

By the end of 1660 choral services had started again but Henry Loosemore the organist used his own chamber organ which he had removed from his rooms and set up in the Chapel for the purpose.

 ". . . .that branching roof self poised, and scooped into ten thousand cells."   *The Times, London*

In due course the main organ was reconstituted. Lancelot Pease undoubtedly worked on the "chaire organ" or choir organ and Thomas Tamar erected the great organ. Tamar was a Peterborough man who resided in Cambridge for the greater part of the period 1660-85 and he had a son in the choir of Trinity College. This instrument was most likely a conglomeration of new and old parts for in 1686 at a cost of £350 Renatus Harris made a considerable amount of basic re-construction upon it. At the next renovation in 1803 by John Avery some of the work was obviously unsatisfactory for the college records indicate that measures were to be taken "to get the organ put in a proper state" and in 1809-10 we learn that £36 was paid to Mr. Elliott, Organ Maker, "for repairing and compleating the organ left unfinished by Avery."

At about this stage Hill and Son the famous organ makers and repairers appear on the scene and they made further improvements in 1834. They continued to work upon it until 1859 when they carried out a complete rebuild. The old case was kept intact although it was doubled in depth from east to west while the keyboards were removed from the east front to the north side where they have remained ever since. Two clumsy Gothic pinnacles which then surmounted the western towers were removed and the present angelic trumpeters set in their place. The story goes that in order to get some idea of how the angels would look "two slender youths" from the college were asked to go and stand on the bases! It seems that there was no lack of volunteers and when one remembers that the exterior of the chapel is a great attraction for the night climbers of Cambridge the keenness of youth to risk its neck in this cause becomes more apparent if less understandable.

In 1876 Messrs Hill cleaned and repaired the organ while in 1888-9 they were carrying out yet another complete rebuild. With one or two exceptions this carries us through to the present day programme of restoration when the organ again came in for its share of attention. This time the object was to brighten the sound of the organ and to improve its tonal balance. In the pedals, for example, this was particularly necessary and the aim was to lighten and improve tonal clarity. The changes in tone were achieved by the removal of seven pipes ranging from sixteen feet to four feet and by substituting six pipes of much shorter length. The longest of these was eight feet and the shortest, two feet in length.

The work was hampered by the extremely tight packing which had gone on in past years as successive organ builders and restorers had tried to fit more and more pipework into a limited space. The public, of course, is now able to judge the changes of tone and sound for itself for apart from the world famous service of lessons and carols which radio and now television take, in a special edited version to all parts of the globe, the choir and organ are heard at all the major festivals of the year.

Although it makes but a silent contribution towards the interior of the Chapel, the case of the organ has been described as "one of our greatest ecclesiastical treasures." Another authority on organ building has written "It is difficult to speak of the case

Hardboard panels protecting both walls and organ screening.

of King's organ save in superlatives. It is generally agreed that although the old Dallam instruments at Worcester Cathedral and St George's Chapel, Windsor, resemble it closely there is really nothing that quite matches it. The carving of the organ case is superb and cunningly carried out. It makes an interesting exercise to stand quietly gazing at the organ case trying to pick out the numerous little carved figures which are to be found at various points. Those in the panels under the pipes of the west case are real works of art. The case work of the instrument is of dark oak but none of the woodwork is gilt with the exception of the trumpets of the two angels standing above the western towers."

The list of organists who have presided at this magnificent instrument throughout the centuries makes interesting reading although it is much too lengthy to discuss in detail in a book of this sort. It contains some famous and interesting names. Edward Gibbons for example who held the office in 1592 was the elder brother of the famous early English composer Orlando Gibbons. Both came from a Cambridge family and Orlando became a choir boy at King's Chapel in his day. Not far from the college is the Fitzwilliam Museum which today houses the famous Fitzwilliam Virginal Book in which much of Orlando Gibbons keyboard work has been preserved. John Tomkins, son of the famous Thomas Tomkins followed Edward Gibbons in 1606. In later years Thomas Tudway held the office although it is on record that he was once suspended for three months for making a pun which was considered disloyal. Tudway was Professor of Music, Composer and Organist Extraordinary to Queen Anne; a superb title if ever I heard one!

CANTA
BRIGIA
qualis extitit,
Anno Dñi
1634

A Caſtellum	P. Coll.S.Iohañis	V.Coll.Corporis Chriſti
B. Ecc. S. Petri	Q. Coll.S.Trinitatis	VI.Ludus Literarius
C. Ecc. S. Egidij	R Aula S.Trinitatis	VII.Ptochotropheiũ
D. Domus Pythagoræ	S Aula Clarenſis	VIII Coll. Reginale
E. Coll. Magdalenæ	T Coll. Gunv. et Caij	IX. Aula S. Catharinæ
F. Ecc.S. Clementis	V. Scholæ Publicæ	X. Ecc S Butolphi
G. Ecc. S Pulchri	W Coll Regale	XI. Aula Pembrochiana
H. Coll. Ieſu	X. Sacellum Regiũ	XII. Domus S. Petri
I. Coll. Sydney	Y. Ecc S Michaelis	XIII. Ecc B Mariæ Minoris
K. Ecc. S. Trinitatis	Z. Ecc B Mariæ	XIV. Granta, ſive
L. Ecc. S. Andreæ	I Ecc S Edvardi	Cham fluvius
M. Coll. Chriſti	II Forum	XV Foſſa Regia
N. Coll. Emañuelis	III Telonium	XVI Runæ Ecc Omniũ
O. Ecc. Omniũ Sanct	IV Ecc S Beñedicti	Sanctorũ ad Caſtrum

TOUT BIEN OU RIEN

Honoratiſsimo Domino Dño
BAPTISTÆ NOEL,
Vicecomiti CAMDEN,
Mecœnati ſuo longe
digniſſimo. &c.

Chapter Eight

IF KING'S College is famous for its Chapel, the Chapel is in turn known throughout the world for its choir. For many people Christmas would not be Christmas if they could not hear the now famous service of Nine Lessons and Carols which is an essential part of Christmas Eve at the College. Measured against the time span of the college and its buildings this famous service is a modern institution, begun as it was by the famous and much revered Dean Milner-White on Christmas Eve, 1918.

Records, radio and now television have taken this incomparable experience to the masses. For example eight million people saw it on television in 1967 and twelve million in 1968 although I must hasten to point out that the television version is not the real thing. Each year the College has had to turn down requests to televise the service 'live' because the very act of staging such a service for television would ruin that indefinable quality which makes the service what it is. A special version therefore is recorded and shown both in England and abroad, whereas sound radio, with its less obtrusive microphones does broadcast the actual service.

I would not like to give the impression that the College is in any way opposed to television or radio. Indeed facilities for running cables inside the Chapel with the minimum of inconvenience and damage to the fabric were built in when the restoration programme was undertaken. The Choir makes a number of very popular long playing records a year and has been doing so for some time. It undertakes foreign tours although Mr David Wilcox, the present choir master and organist, explains that "it is our main job to be here, we only go off for very short periods during vacations." Visitors to the College expect to be able to hear the choir in the Chapel and their wishes help to prevent the choir from undertaking a long tour of America and Canada, to which countries it is always being invited. All this tends to sidetrack attention from the main role of the choir which is to sing at the daily services during the periods of the university term and at the major festivals. Nor should it be forgotten that the choristers and choral scholars are pursuing normal educational courses in addition to their choral duties.

Foreign tours are a long standing institution with the Choir but because of the problems I have outlined they have to be of fairly short duration. Switzerland, Germany, Holland are typical of countries which have been visited and which are close enough to be encompassed without upsetting the choir's home commitments. Visitors who enter the Chapel purely to hear the choir sing are not restricted to the summer months. Just as many arrive during the winter and these, I should imagine, will be delighted by the new under floor heating described earlier.

To those associated with the choir the fame of the Christmas Eve service has become a little irritating because it tends to place undue emphasis on what is after

Bird's-eye view of Cambridge, from Thomas Fuller's History of the University. Note, as in all maps in this book, the bell tower at the end of the Chapel. The site of this still shows up on modern aerial photographs. *Reproduced by kind permission of Cambridge University Library*

Modern choirboys in traditional dress.   *Alfred Hepworth, London*

all but one service throughout a busy year. Even so I don't think it is out of place to recall for a moment just how this Festival of Nine Lessons and Carols came about, for already there are the signs that it is becoming the model for an increasing number of similar services in other parts of the globe. Dean Milner-White was appointed to office at the age of thirty four and it was his experiences as an Army chaplain in the First World War which convinced him that the Church of England needed more imaginative worship. For example he devised King's Advent Carol Service in 1934 and was a liturgical pioneer and authority during his 25 years as Dean of York. The Service in 1918 began with an invitatory carol, 'Up, Good Christian Folk' before the hymn "Once in Royal David's City" and the Magnificat formed the climax. In fact that experiment of fifty years ago was in turn based on an order drawn up by E. W. Benson, who was later to become Archbishop of Canterbury, for use in the wooden shed which then served as his cathedral in Truro. That particular service was held at 10 p.m. on Christmas Eve 1880.

A. C. Benson recalled "My father arranged from ancient sources a little service for Christmas Eve—nine carols and nine tiny lessons, which were read by various officers of the Church beginning with a chorister, and ending, through the different grades, with a Bishop." The suggestion had come from G. M. S. Walpole, later Bishop of Edinburgh.

In 1918 it was explained at King's that the new service "was intended to symbolise the loving bond between the two Foundations of Henry VI here and at Eton, the

Massed choirs traverse the Great Court of King's College for a Festival in the Chapel.
Cambridge Evening News

goodwill between University and Town and peace within the whole Church of the Lord Jesus, as well as the joy and worship of us all at the coming of our Christ."

The service was first broadcast in 1928 and it was from this period that the present fame of the service and its popularity began to grow. With the exception of 1929 the service has been broadcast each year, even throughout the Second World War when the glass, and the heating, had been removed and the name of the Chapel could not be mentioned for security reasons. Perhaps it played a more important part then than many people realised, for there is nothing quite so effective in restoring one's faith in the world, and in oneself, as the Christmas Eve service at King's Chapel. To visitors harrassed by the war years it must have formed a valuable island of peace and of timelessness.

Since 1963 a shorter and more informal service has also been transmitted on television and largely as the result of these broadcasts and the growth of long playing records made by the choir—some four or five each year—churches throughout the world have been encouraged to adapt the form of the service for their Christmas celebrations. Dean Milner-White, however, issued a warning to anyone who found themselves tempted to substitute more carols than lessons. "It's liturgical order and

King's College Choir in 1897. A. E. Brooke, Junior Dean, fourth from right in second row, was uncle of Rupert Brooke the poet.

The famous Choir gathered for the Christmas Service of Lessons and Carols. Note the extensive heraldic decoration incorporated by Henry VII. *Cambridge Evening News*

pattern is the strength of the service; the main theme is the development of the loving purpose of God from the Creation to the Incarnation through the windows and words of the Bible; the scriptures, not the carols, are the backbone."

New carols have been introduced nearly every year by successive organists at the Chapel. "Daddy" Mann, Boris Ord, Harold Darke, Mr Ord's substitute during the war, and Mr David Willcox, a pupil of Boris Ord and now his successor. "In Dulci Jubilo" has however, been sung every year and was a firm favourite as far back as 1918. For the first Christmas Eve since the restoration of the Chapel a further innovation was tried. A choral celebration of Holy Communion was held at 11.30 on Christmas Eve. The music was sung by men's voices only and the service, although not intended to be 'popular' was open to the public.

With the exception of one period when choral services at the Chapel were supressed by the Puritans, the choir has been singing services continuously for over 500 years. The choir is of course, older than the building itself and was established when Henry VI founded the College in 1441. It consisted of six lay clerks to sing the male voice parts and sixteen boy choristers to sing the treble parts and in addition there were to be ten chaplains. These were to be trained singers with good voices and it is likely that when necessary they reinforced the lay clerks in singing the services while a chaplain or lay clerk acted as organist.

More than seventy years before the present chapel was finished the choir was singing the services in a temporary chapel and this they continued to do until 1536 when the great new Chapel became ready. It is recorded that one evening after vespers the temporary chapel fell to the ground, rather as if it knew that its task was finished. The composition of the choir has changed somewhat over the years although the basic form remains much as it was. During the time of Elizabeth I the number of chaplains was cut down from ten to three and today there are usually two. Between 1880 and 1928 the old lay clerks, who were professional singers, were gradually replaced by choral scholars who are undergraduate members of the College studying for degrees. They sing all the male voice parts.

The organist is now a Fellow of the College and since 1930 he has been assisted by an undergraduate organ student. In spite of all the changes, however, the number of the choristers has remained unchanged since the fifteenth century. It was fixed at sixteen by Henry in 1453 and it is sixteen to this day. Today it is also one of the most famous choirs in Europe and one of the principal choirs of the world, a choir with a very distinctive balance and tone of its own.

Chapter Nine

IT HAS always seemed to me that one cannot discuss the choir of King's College Chapel without looking at the background and history of King's College School. This must be one of the oldest Preparatory Schools in England for it was founded by Henry VI when he founded the College and today it is a fine school in its own right for which the demand always exceeds the available number of places.

The site adjoins the grounds of the University Library and is bounded on two sides by West Road and Grange Road. The fact that it is built upon a gravel soil has long been considered particularly healthy and today the school shows signs of considerable extension and modernisation with a superb hall, laboratories, a swimming pool and playing fields of considerable charm and atmosphere. It remains within walking distance of the College and this is most important from the point of view of the boys in the choir who regularly make the journey on foot and who provide one of the traditional sights of Cambridge as they wend their way through 'The Backs' dressed on occasions in Eton Suits and silk hats.

Visitors to Cambridge frequently find themselves completely mystified by the role of the school. I have heard Americans assure one another that it exists simply to educate the sixteen members of the choir! This may have been so in its early history but it seems likely that the arrangement became that of other endowed schools where the headmaster taught the boys on the foundation free of charge but was able to augment his income by taking in other boys. These would have been day boys and in its early days the school was directed by its Founder to take choristers of honest conversation and under twelve years old! Originally the boys were drawn from the lower classes of Cambridge boys who were looked after, clothed and educated by the College. This was the system until 1876, the date of the foundation of the present school, and the time at which the College undertook to reform the musical services at the Chapel and to build the choir school.

Today the school contains about 180 boys of whom 16 are choristers, and 8 probationer choristers. About 95 are day boys, many sons of members of the university, and the remainder are boarders. Classes are of about 17 boys each, a figure which must be the envy of educational establishments of all types throughout the country. Between three and five probationer choristers are elected by open competition each year, and although the majority of candidates come from the United Kingdom, there are occasional competitors from overseas. The earliest age at which a boy can be accepted for trial is around his eighth birthday, while the age of ten is usually considered "elderly" in this context. An ear for music and good voice are obviously essential and if the boy can play an instrument this is taken into account. His preliminary examination consists of reading English prose, a voice test for quality and compass and oral tests which

The School in 1905.

include accurate pitching of single notes, distinguishing the notes of simple chords and the singing of simple tunes played first on the piano. Later, for those who progress beyond the preliminary stages, there is an educational test and the singing of a hymn of the boy's own choice.

Even though he has been awarded a probationer choristership a boy does not immediately don an angelic look and a surplice and start singing in the Chapel as some visitors seem to imagine. He enters the school and attends all daily practices held at the school but will not normally sing in the choir of Kings' until a chorister vacancy occurs. He will then enter the choir as a chorister-elect and after a year with the choir will be required to pass a second trial. Then, and only then, if conduct, progress in school work and progress at music are all of a sufficient standard the boy's election to a choristership is confirmed. He will be expected to learn the piano and will receive an initial grant towards the cost of his Eton suit and silk hat.

There are normally only four weekday services and so the choristers miss little in the way of education and games from their singing. They might in addition play in one of the two orchestras of 30 players, each of which rehearses once a week. The boys may also be found in the music room or music practice rooms, the school library, the art room, the sculpture room, or even the photographic dark room, printing room or model railway room. Such facilities are very far removed from the conditions of the original school and the boys who were members of it.

The site of the original school seems to be lost in antiquity and while many historians have hazarded guesses a firm decision seems to have eluded us. The first master over the choristers whose name has come down to us was a Mr Brantham who was certainly teaching them in 1456. John Saltmarsh, the historian of King's College, is of the opinion that he was probably Robert Brantham who had been a King's scholar at Eton and for a short time, scholar at King's. In 1456 Brantham was one of the lay clerks who sang male voice parts in the choir before the days of the choral scholars.

As one comes forward in time details of the school and its buildings become clearer. In 1693 for example, the college put up a new building near its present main gate and it stood until the present screen was built in the 1820's. The northern half of the ground floor of this building was originally a school for the choristers and consisted of one big room in which they took their lessons together. If anyone cares to look closely at the lawn in very dry weather, picking a spot just north of the cobbles leading to the front gate, markings of the foundations can be seen and measured. The brickwork is only a few inches below the surface and in dry weather the grass above it withers and turns brown marking out the original plans quite distinctly. Measurements show that the schoolroom was much larger than it need have been for sixteen boys and this suggests that boys other than choristers had already begun to attend the school. Prior to this it is likely that the boys were taught in one of the old houses in King's Parade which had been converted into College buildings in the fifteenth century.

Life for choristers in Elizabethan times was hard. In addition to services, practices and lessons they were expected to wait in hall as well. Punishments were harsh, whipping and birching were common, and the rules of the College were strict. It was Provost Goad who in 1571 made a rule forbidding any member of the College to go swimming. If a chorister or undergraduate was caught he was given a severe whipping in front of the whole College, although I have no doubt that the punishment lent additional excitement to the inevitable illegal bathing expeditions which must have been organised. Senior members of the College caught bathing were sentenced to sit in the stocks all day.

The 1691 brick building became part of the Provost's Lodge in 1786 and we do not know what happened to the choristers and their school. We do know that a schoolrooms was provided when William Wilkins designed his building in 1823. Wilkins designed the Hall range and the screen wall which is visible from King's Parade today. He provided a school room for the choristers behind the west end of the hall on the ground floor and looking out onto the kitchen yard. Thirty years later however, it looks as though their schoolroom was the room subsequently used as the kitchen office which is half way up the stairs to the gallery.

For an interesting first hand account of the school at this period we can again return to "Memoirs of a Kings College Chorister" by Thomas Case which was published in 1899 but which relates to a period some sixty years before. He recalls that the attention given to "high class manners" among the boys was based on what happened at their dinner table. The table was set in their schoolroom "which was over the butteries"* and each boy would have a lump of bread placed before him, was lucky if he saw two vegetables as well as meat, and consumed beer from a drinking horn! Salt was provided and so was mustard on special days but the boys were expected to bring their own pepper.

Of course choristers were expected to wait at a table upon Fellows and other senior members of the College and it was not unknown for a lad with a healthy appetite to spirit away some of the more choice cuts of meat or fowl for his own private consumption. The master of the school, according to Case, "was also the butler of Clare Hall College, rather aged and somewhat asthmatical, not over strict. . . . . . ." Thomas Case also provides a glimpse of the less pleasurable side to singing in the choir of the Chapel. He and the other boys would certainly have appreciated the modern underfloor heating, for Case recalls that it was often so cold in the Chapel that because he was of a weakly disposition he would regularly faint and would have to be carried to his home which was fortunately nearby.

Of the Chapel he adds "I wonder how many of my readers have upon a lovely sunshiny Sunday afternoon gazed through and beyond the stately open west doors, the west end being made more glorious since the stained glass window above has been presented and fixed. It must to a sound mind constrain the thoughts to 'How wonderful are Thy works, in wisdom hast Thou made them all; the Earth is full of thy riches,' and as long as the organ is sending forth its notes it has a measure of fascination, or should I not say inspiration, that seems to hold one to the spot."

The reference to the west window "presented and fixed" is to the work of Clayton and Bell who were responsible for the great west window, "The Last Judgement" in 1879. Case rounds off his little soliloquy to the Chapel with a line which I fancy is engraved upon the hearts of all Kings choirboys. "Dear old King's Chapel, would God that every undevout incident connected could be entirely obliterated, and every Heavenly and good one be immovably grafted in my very being."

It was not until the reorganisation of the school in 1876 that boarders arrived on the scene. The first three were accommodated in a boarding house at 3 Pemberton Terrace behind Brookside, a fair walk from the College, and here the Rev. H. T. Biscoe, one of the Chaplains, looked after them. Meanwhile a new schoolhouse was being built in the Paddocks behind the Fellows' Garden where the Fellows' horses were kept, which is where the school stands today. In the Michaelmas Term of 1878 the school reopened in its new buildings under the first of its modern headmasters, the Reverend V. C. R. Reynell of Trinity Hall.

And so we return to the present school. There has been considerable progress since the school moved into its "new buildings" in 1878. Today the matured red brick

---

*Places within Colleges where provisions, including ale, are kept.

is a constant reminder of the school's traditions and its past, and there are newer and later buildings to carry everyone into the future. A new assembly hall was completed in 1963, a large and well equipped science laboratory was built in 1965 and further buildings including class rooms, a projector room and two music rooms are to be completed shortly.

Let me end this chapter on the school and its occupants by quoting from an excellent article on the school which appeared many years ago in the "Cathedral Quarterly." "Take it altogether, the lot of the King's Chorister is a happy one. He gets none too much Chapel, a delightfully situated school, plenty of fresh air as well as good holidays; and it is always with regret that a boy sees his days numbered owing to the fact that his voice is sinking to the abyss, whence it may or may not rise again."

Headmaster Benjamin Benham and the King's College Choir School cricket team in 1894.

Chapter Ten

I SUGGESTED in an earlier chapter that few people bother to discuss something which fails to interest them, and that at a somewhat higher level controversy can often be regarded as a direct measure of affection. It was to be expected therefore, that almost as soon as the renovation scheme had reached a state of finality that discussion and indeed controversy came following on behind.

In this Chapter I have endeavoured to present, as fairly as possibly, the lines that the discussion took as it appeared in the correspondence columns of the national and provincial press, and in other publications. I do so for this reason. During the course of one's researches for a book of this kind I have time and time again found myself reading about the construction and alteration, not only of King's College Chapel but other important buildings as well, and I have always found myself wondering about the reaction of people at the time. One learns so much more about the problems, the attitudes, the prejudices and the state of the political and social climate of an age from an insight into its feelings that I feel the reaction to the scheme at King's has a part to play in this. In subsequent years somebody might look at this volume or at the original correspondence and find themselves amused by our earnest concern with this or baffled by our applause for that. Almost certainly the Chapel will be available to them for first hand study, unless a nuclear holocaust has blasted it out of existence, in which case neither book, correspondence nor Chapel, will be of much concern to anyone.

But let us look on the bright side. Let us assume with all hope that the serene and masterly form will still dominate the Cambridge skyline as it has done for so many hundreds of years. Let us also assume that the future students of the building will be interested in the schemes carried out during our own age for which we may be cursed or praised—who can tell?

The Cross, or rather its absence, and the setting of the altar really formed the centrepiece of the discussion. It was argued that the efforts to produce a suitable setting for the "Adoration of the Magi" and which has resulted in the lowering of the floor had also detracted from the true stature and symbolical significance of the altar. One leading churchman argued that the painting had in fact taken the place of the cross on the altar and suggested that the whole treatment was a symbol of the secularisation of the interior of many churches which was occurring today. "Is it right" he asked "to subordinate liturgical function to aesthetic effect?"

Whatever the substance of this argument, it was a little premature at the time it was advanced. It was true that at the time there was not a cross on the altar in the position churchgoers have long expected it to be. But although the scheme was completed in its broadest outline it had by no means reached finality in detail for many months after the Chapel was reopened to the public. I spoke to Sir Martyn Beckett at about this time and on this very point and he told me that he was still giving serious

In the spring each year the walk across "The Backs" to the Chapel is bounded by myriads of daffodils and crocuses.
Cambridge Evening News

A sketch made by Sir Martyn Beckett of one of the rejected ideas for the siting of Ruben's picture.

consideration to the question of the cross and had in fact produced a number of suitable designs which were to be tried upon the altar. One of these, a simple cross of ebony and gold, was in fact accepted and its manufacture put in hand.

There is, as other correspondents hastened to point out, an enormous cross in the stained glass of the east window directly above both picture and altar. Not only that but the superb new altar cloth designed by Joyce Conway Evans and made by Edinburgh Weavers, also contains the cross as its principal motif. One university Don, who was by no means adulatory about the scheme dismissed the argument about the cross as "rather trivial" and went on to point out that in the Elizabethan age Communion tables lacked such crosses as did the altar of Magdalen College, Oxford in the early eighteenth century.

Whether or not the cross controversy concerns the reader will largely depend upon his own religious background and the influences to which he has been subjected. But the second main point of controversy however, is one which any visitor with a sense of the artistic might like to weigh up for himself, for I am personally convinced that the answer in this case lies very much in the eye of the beholder. This discussion hinges around the advisability of putting Rubens' painting in the east end of the Chapel at all. Some correspondents put the point firmly but politely. Others were more outspoken. This extract, I think, comes from the first school: "King's is supremely English perpendicular which correctly interpreted (and where better exemplified than here) means poetry in soaring structural stonework with magnificent infill panels of stained glass, often in tremendous proportions.

"Clearly the amount of plain wall space for a painting such as Rubens' is strictly limited, as opposed to a large amount of wall space in the case of Roman Churches where full rein may be given to wall frescoes, and indeed such wall spaces have been a back-cloth for Giotto, Fra Angelico, Michaelangelo and many others. King's, Cambridge, however, is not a Padua, Florence or Rome—therein lies the rub. Might it not be that Rubens is wrongly sited? The problem of the altar cross and Rubens remains. Should Rubens be housed in a new contemporary annexe?"

Obviously the protagonists were not afraid to fling in their own highly original suggestions. If fitting the Rubens into the Chapel posed such problems I personally quaver at the thought of tacking on a whole new contemporary annexe and the arguments which would accompany it! But let us turn to another critic who put the point about the painting more vehemently.

"It is regrettable that the redecorators of King's should have wedged between window and altar a second painted reredos by Rubens not designed for any place like this Chapel. It should, of course, dominate some lofty Baroque altarpiece but is instead depressed by a window of incomparable date and style. To accommodate the Rubens physically, the sanctuary floor, which should be three feet above that of the Choir, has been lowered considerably. Contrast the Founder's wishes as printed in Willis and Clark. Moreover it was found necessary by the architect of the scheme, who seems to follow the notorious Lord Grimthorpe, to clear away all the beautiful panelling which was introduced only some 60 years ago, but which after four centuries at first gave it the warmth and life it had always craved. The Chapel now reverts to frigidity. But lest the Rubens, without its proper surround and set against a bare wall should suggest a shaving mirror in a bathroom, it has been mocked up as a triptych of sub-mediaeval style, with two bogus side panels. To aggravate the discord, the new altar frontal suggests a bad copy of a fifteenth century Italian ceiling. . . ."

And so on and so on.

Just how typical this view might be one can assess by quoting a further correspondent on the same subject of the altar cloth. "This is surely an outstanding piece of contemporary cloth work and it is delicious." Clearly time and age have some healing work to do before Cambridge ever sees eye to eye with itself over the subject of King's Chapel.

The liturgical criticisms were duly answered by the then Dean of the Chapel, the Reverend D. L. Edwards who told journalists when they visited the building that liturgical considerations had been very carefully assessed when the new scheme was being designed. As a result it was now possible for a priest to move around the altar whereas this had not been possible before. He emphasised that the symbol of the cross remained in the east window and on the altar cloth.

The third main point of discussion is that touched on in an earlier chapter by Sir Martyn Beckett himself, the problem of a glass window of one colour surmounting a painting which exhibits a different set of colours and values. Reaction here seems to have been almost equally divided, among those who have actually taken the trouble to visit the Chapel and look, that is. A salient factor of the Chapel is the manner in which many people who know it well are prepared to advance views without ever bothering to study the finished scheme. Some visitors do find the proximity of the painting and the east window bothers them. Others accept the view of the architect that one cannot in fact focus on the two at once and therefore any direct conflict is a physiological impossibility.

Certainly the man who wrote to say that he considered the restored Chapel "looked magnificent" but if the Rubens was moved a little to the right "as far as the Fitzwilliam Museum" it would look better, obviously did not subscribe to the physiological impossibility theory! All this discussion can really only mean one thing. I have hoped throughout the writing of this book that the few facts presented here will inspire the reader to visit the Chapel and immerse himself in its atmosphere. I am sure that if he is arriving for the first time he will be entering upon an experience which will remain with him for a lifetime. Once he has exposed himself to the atmosphere, the colour and the all embracing serenity of what must be one of man's finest architectural achievements in the world he will equally certainly wish to return, often again and again.

Did those craftsmen of so long ago really arrive at such perfect proportions and such soaring unity of style without divine guidance? Outside King's College Chapel, Cambridge, in the clarity of daylight it is easy to be objective.

But once inside it is difficult to be so certain.

An interim scheme for the east end of the Chapel also later rejected. Sir Martyn Beckett is seated in the foreground.

Cambridge Evening News

APPENDIX A

Details of Stained Glass Windows
King's College Chapel.

Starting from the north west corner the pictures run as follows: one, is top left; two, bottom left; three, top right and four, bottom right.

Window

A 1. Joachim's offering rejected.
   2. Joachim and Anna at the Golden Gate of the Temple.
   3. An Angel bids him return to Jerusalem.
   4. Birth of the Virgin.

B. 1. Presentation of the Golden Table in the Temple of the Sun.
   2. Presentation of the Virgin.
   3. Marriage of Tobias and Sara.
   4. Marriage of Joseph and Mary.

C. 1. Eve tempted.
   2. The Annunciation.
   3. The Burning Bush.
   4. The Birth of Jesus Christ.

D. 1. The Circumcision of Isaac.
   2. The Circumcision of Christ.
   3. The Queen of Sheba visits Solomon.
   4. The Adoration of the Magi. (Window panel, not painting.)

E. 1. Purification of women under the law.
   2. Presentation of Christ in the Temple.
   3. Jacob's flight from Esau.
   4. The flight into Egypt.

F. 1. The Golden Calf.
   2. The Idols of Egypt falling.
   3. Massacre of the seed royal by Athalia.
   4. Massacre of the innocents.

G. 1. Naaman washing in Jordan.
   2. The Baptism of Christ.
   3. Jacob tempts Esau to sell his Birthright.
   4. Christ tempted by Satan.

H. 1. Elisha raising the Shunamite's son.
   2. The raising of Lazarus.
   3. David's triumph after slaying Goliath.
   4. Christ's entry into Jerusalem.

I. 1. The Manna falling from Heaven.
   2. The Last Supper.
   3. The Fall of the Rebel Angels.
   4. The agony in the garden.

J. 1. Cain killing Abel.
   2. The betrayal.
   3. Shimei cursing David.
   4. Christ mocked.

K. 1. Jerimiah imprisoned.
   2. Christ before Annas.
   3. The shame of Noah.
   4. Christ before Herod.

L. 1. Job tormented.
   2. Christ scourged.
   3. Solomon crowned.
   4. Christ crowned with thorns.

The east end of King's College Chapel with the Adoration of the Magi sited as visitors now will see it. The light units take both the smokeless candles and electric light.   *Cambridge Evening News*

M.   1. Christ nailed to the cross.
(The East Window)
2. The Crucifixion.
3. The Deposition.

3. Ecce homo.
4. Pilate washing his hands.
5. Christ bearing the cross.

N.   1. and 3. Moses and the Brazen serpent (by Hedgeland 1845).
2. Naomi and her daughters-in-law
bewailing Elimelech.

4. Christ bewailed.

O.   1. Joseph cast into the pit.
2. The entombment.

3. The Exodus.
4. The Harrowing of Hell.

P.   1. Jonah cast up by the whale.
2. The Resurrection.

3. Tobias returning to his mother.
4. Christ appearing to the Virgin.

Q.   1. Reuben seeks Joseph.
2. The three Marys at the Sepulchre.

3. Darius finds Daniel alive in the Den of
Lions.
4. Christ recognised by St Mary Magadalene.

R.   1. The Angel Raphael meets Tobias.
2. Christ on the way to Emmaus.

3. Habbakuk feeding Daniel in the Den.
4. The Supper at Emmaus.

S.   1. The return of the prodigal son.
2. The Incredulity of St Thomas.

3. The meeting of Joseph and Jacob.
4. Christ appearing to the Apostles.

T.   1. Elijah carried up to Heaven.
2. The Ascension.

3. Moses receives the Law.
4. The Descent of the Holy Spirit.

U.   1. St Peter and St John heal the lame man.
2. St Peter and the Apostles going to the
Temple.

3. The Apostles arrested.
4. The death of Ananias.

V.   1. The Conversion of St Paul.
2. St Paul and St Barnabas at Lystra.

3. St Paul at Damascus.
4. St Paul stoned at Lystra.

W.   1. St Paul at Philippi exorcises the woman
with the spirit of divination.
2. St Paul saying farewell at Philippi.

3. St Paul before the Chief Captain Lysias.
4. St Paul before Nero.

X.   1. The death of Tobit.
2. The death of the Virgin.

3. The burial of Jacob.
4. The funeral of the Virgin.

Y.   1. The translation of Enoch.
2. The Assumption of the Virgin.

3. Solomon and Bath-sheba.
4. The Coronation of the Virgin.

Z.   (The West Window) The Last Judgement by Clayton and Bell, 1879.

INDEX

93

G

Genuynge, Magister, 69.
Germany, 73.
Gibbons — Edward, 71.
        — Orlando, 71.
Gibbs building, 48, 53.
Giotto, 87.
Goad, Provost Roger, 69, 81.
Gog Magog Hills, 13.
Gonville, Edmund, 15.
Gonville and Caius, 15.
Goodchild, Michael, 9.
Grange Road, 79.
Grimthorpe, Lord, 87.

H

Hardwick, Roy, 8, 39, 40, 42.
Harris, Renatus, 70.
Hartop, 69.
Henry VI, 13, 15-17, 19, 46, 51, 75.
        — "Will", 13, 37, 53, 78, 79, 87.
Henry VII, 20, 39, 44, 53, 55.
Henry VIII, 53, 57.
Heraldic — antelope, 53.
        — beasts, 39, 44, 53.
        — crowns, 39, 55.
        — dragon, 39, 53, 55.
        — emblem, 53.
        — Fleur-de-lys, 39, 55.
        — greyhound, 39, 53, 55.
        — lion, 53.
        — portcullis, 44, 55.
        — Royal Arms, 55.
        — Tudor rose, 44 55.
Hill and Son, 70.
Hitler, 64.
Holland, 73.
Honorary M.A., 58.
Hone, Galyon, 64.
Houses of Parliament, 29.
Huddleston, 16.
Hygrometers, 42.

I

Italy, 48.

K

King, Dennis, 8, 42, 61, 63.
King's Advent Carol Service, 74.
King's Cliffe, 17.

King's College — advisors, 37; assistance, 8; boys education, 79; Committee, 26, 27, 29, 32; cost to, 22, 67; early title, 15; Eton scholars, 16; Fellow of, 78; foundation, 15; grand design for, 13; Great Court, 16, 51, 53; heating, 27; Historian, 53, 81; library, 8; members of, 20, 29; Our Lady, 65; Rector to Provost, 16; Richard III, 19, 20; rules, 81; scheme, 8; visitors, 73.

King's College Chapel — air, 42; Altar piece, 34; at its finest, 12; atmosphere, 26; bay, 39, 43, 61; builders, 13, 22; candles, 22, 23, 27, 41; Choir, 8, 67, 73-78, 87; Choirboy, 71, 82; "Church in the round", 32; cleaning, 39, 40; completion, 8, 10; controversy, 33, 85, 88; craftsmen, 55; Dean of, 63, 88; drains outside, 40; early design, 17; east end, 8, 31, 32, 51, 56, 87; faces, 55; fan vault, 34, 48, 54; first view of, 51; floor, 27, 29, 37, 45, 48, 49; fabric, 29; gantry, 39, 43; glass and stone, 11, 43; Gothic, 34; heating, 27, 37, 46, 48, 76; height, 40; history, 8, 22; imposing mass of, 29; impression, 13; interior, 27; landmark, 15; lofty vault, 31; layout, 32; magnificence, 34; needs of, 37; organ, 27, 31, 34, 42, 46, 49, 55-57, 67, 69, 71; Our Lady, 65; perspective, 11; protective work, 39; radio and T.V., 73; restoration, 42, 58; Royal visit, 67, 69; side chapel, 52, 63; south side, 16, 51; south west door, 31; stability, 46; staff, 8, 31; stone, 16, 45; temporary chapel, 78; temporary entrance, 52; unfinished pile, 19; visit to, 51; visitors, 12, 22, 31, 35, 73; west end, 53, 55; windows, 8, 34, 42, 49, 61-66, 76, 82, 91, 92.
King's College Choir School, 9, 79-83.
King's Glazier, 64.
Kings of Norwich, 8.
King's Parade, 53, 65, 81.

L

Lavenham, 20.
Leigh, Edward, 9.
Leigh, Rev. Augustus Austen, 12, 13.
Lincoln Cathedral, 31.
London, 57, 58, 69; airport, 31; East End, 23.
Louvain, White Sisters of, 57.

M

Madingley Hill, 13.
Magdalen College, 87.
Maguire and Murray, 31.
Mann, Dr, 67, 77.
Marble — black, 48, 49.
        — white, 48, 49.
Master Mason, 17, 18, 20, 52.
Memoirs of a King's College Chorister, 67, 81.
Michaelangelo, 87.
Michael House, 15.

Millington, William, 15.
Milner-White, Dean, 63, 73, 74, 76.
Milne Street, 15.

N

National Gallery, Director of, 33.
Nicholas, St., 15.
Nicholson, James, 64.
Norman Castle, 15.
Northamptonshire, 16, 17, 44.
Norwich, 8, 61, 64.

O

Ord, Boris, 77.
Organ, 27, 31, 34, 42, 46, 49, 55-57.
Oxford, 16, 33, 87.

P

Paddocks, 82.
Padua, 87.
Pease, Lancelot, 70.
Pemberton Terrace, 82.
Peterborough, 70.
Pevsner, Professor Nicholas, 33.
Pratt, John, 67.
Prentice, Martin, 52.
Preparatory School, 79.
Professor of Music, Composer and Organist
    Extraordinary, 71.
Provost's Lodge, 81.
Puritans, 64, 78.

Q

Queen's Commissioners, 69.
Queen's Lane, 15.
Queen's Pictures, Surveyor of the, 33.

R

Ramsey and Muspratt, 9.
Ramsey, Dean, 63.
Rattee and Kett, 8, 29, 39, 44.
Redman, John, 9.
Reeve, Thomas, 64.
Reynell, Rev. V. C. R., 82.
Reynolds, Sir Joshua, 57.
Richard III, 19, 51, 53.
Roman Churches, 87.
Rome, 87.
Rosser and Russell, 27, 46.

Royal Commission on Historical Monuments, 9.
Rubens, 12, 22, 26, 27, 31, 32, 34, 37, 42, 46,
    48, 49, 55, 57-59, 87, 88.
Russell, David, 27, 46.

S

Saffron Walden Church, 20.
St Albans, Battle of, 19.
St George's — Chapel, 71.
            — Day, 20.
St James Day, 16.
St Pauls, 29.
Saltmarsh, John, 54, 55, 81.
Scandinavia, 22, 23.
Semark, Henry, 20.
Service of Lessons and Carols, 39, 48, 70, 73, 74,
    76, 77.
Shakesperean, 69.
Skeaping, J. R., R. A., 31.
Soane Museum, 33.
Southwark, 64.
Sudbury, 20.
Suffolk, 20.
Summerson, Sir John, 33.
Swedish, 23.
Switzerland, 73.
Symondes, Symond, 64.

T

Tadcaster, 16.
Tamar, Thomas, 70.
Thames, 15.
Thefdale, 16.
Tibbs, Rodney, 11.
Times, The, 9.
Tomkins — John, 71.
            — Thomas, 71.
Trinity — College, 15, 70.
            — Hall, 15, 82.
            — Street, 13.
Truro Cathedral, 74.
Tudway, Thomas, 71.

U

United Kingdom, 63, 79.
United States, 31.
University Hall, 15.

V

Vacuum cleaner, 39, 40.
Vellert, Dirick, 64.
Victoria, Queen, 67.
Virgin Mary and St Nicholas, College of, 15.
Voyage Pittoresque de la Flandre, 57.

W

Wallace Collection, 57.
Walpole, G. M. S., 75.
Walpole, Horace, 37.
Wars of the Roses, 19.
Wastell, John, 11, 20, 53, 55, 67.
Westminster, Duke of, 58.
West Road, 79.
White City, 55.
White Sisters of Louvain, 57.
Wilcox, David, 73, 77.
Wilkins, William, 81.
William of Wykeham, 16.
Williamson, Francis, 64.
Willis and Clark, 87.
Winchester, 16, 61.

Windsor, 71.
Woolrich, John, 17.
Worcester Cathedral, 71.
Wordsworth, 12.
World War — I, 46, 48, 63, 74.
　　　　　 — II, 13, 26, 63, 64, 76.
Wren, Sir Christopher, 37.
Wroxham Hall, 63.

Y

York — Dean of, 74.
　　　 — Minster, 13, 16.
　　　 — Stone, 46.
Yorkshire, 16, 44.

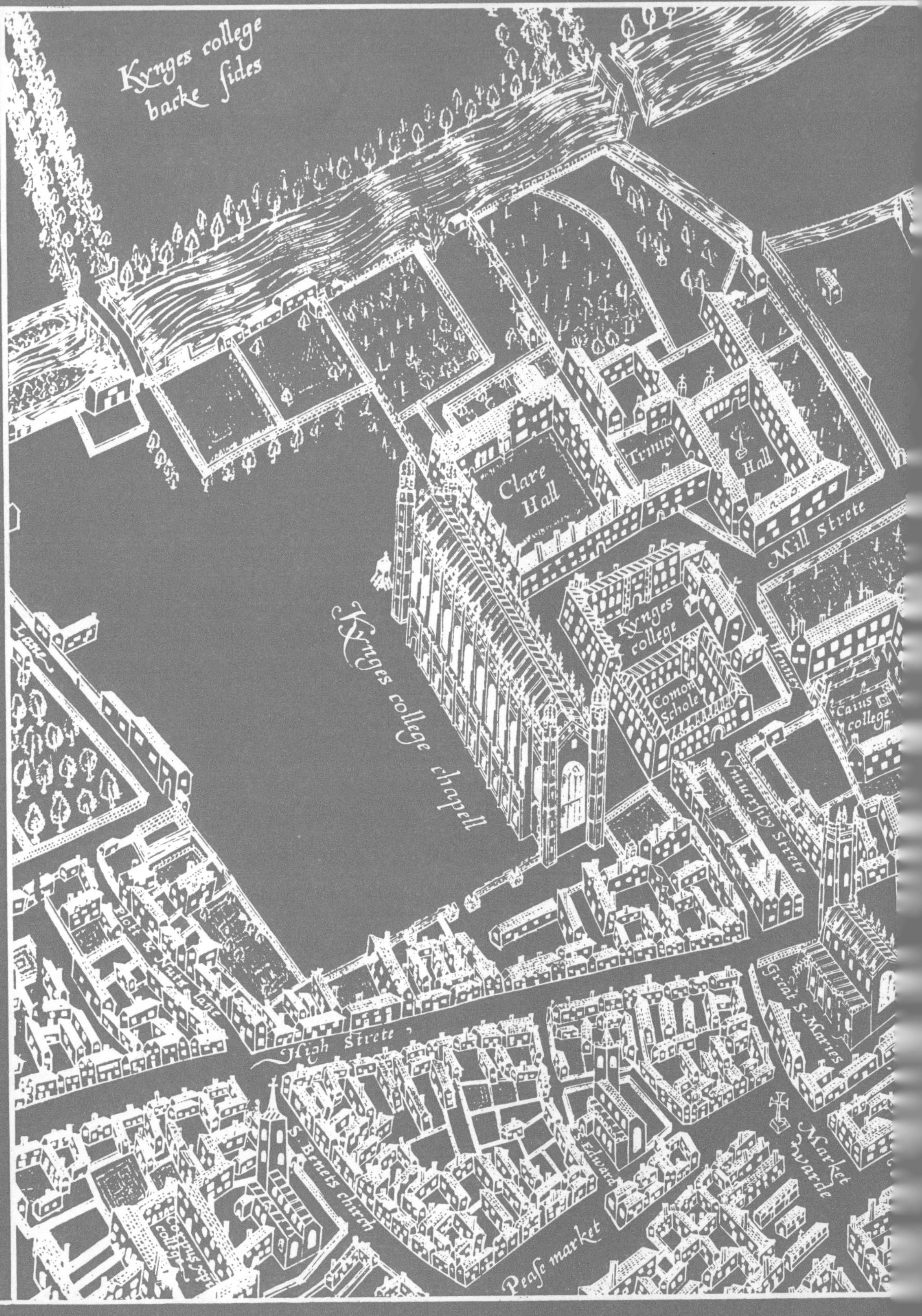
Kynges college backe sides
Clare Hall
Trinity Hall
Mill strete
Kynges college
Comon Schole
Caius college
Kynges college chapell
Vniuersity strete
Lane
Plott & Nutts lane
High Strete
Great S Maries
Market warde
S Benets church
Edward
Pease market

Central Sheet of the bird's-eye view of Cambridge, measured and drawn by JOHN HAMMOND *of Clare Hall, and dated 22 February, 1592.*